MY LIFE

Mrs Annie S. Swan

MY LIFE

An Autobiography

BY

ANNIE S. SWAN

MCMXXXIV

IVOR NICHOLSON & WATSON, LTD.

44 ESSEX STREET, STRAND, LONDON, W.C.2

First Edition (5000 Copies) . . . September 1934
Reprinted (2000 Copies) . . . . October 1934
    ,,   (2000 Copies) . . . .   ,,   1934
    ,,   (5000 Copies) . . . .   ,,   1934
    ,,   (3000 Copies) . . . November 1934
    ,,   (3000 Copies) . . . December 1934
    ,,   (3000 Copies) . . .   ,,   1934

PRINTED IN GREAT BRITAIN BY
MORRISON AND GIBB LTD., LONDON AND EDINBURGH

TO

EFFIE

"Belovèd, strong and stedfast like the hills,
Soft as the summer seas, brave to endure;
In peace or war, great comrade, full equipt!"

FOREWORD

I HAVE quite frequently said that I would never write anything in the shape of an autobiography. But when pressure from various quarters was brought to bear upon me, I began to wonder whether, after all, some part of my experience, faithfully recorded, might not be of interest and value to others.

Two handicaps faced me at the very beginning. First, the absence of any diaries or copious notes. I had nothing therefore to draw upon except a rather inadequate memory, and some valued letters which had been preserved rather by good luck than serious intent.

Those who know me best will not be in the least surprised at this : they have often rebuked me for being too prodigal of everything, all my days.

The second handicap is that in a book of this kind the Ego, which I don't very much like, must of necessity abound.

If one starts to write the story of one's life, well, it *is* the story of one's life, not another's.

Its chief value, if any, is the testimony it bears

regarding the things I have found most worth while in life.

I give it with my love and gratitude, and without a qualm, to the large public which has so loyally supported me for half a century.

ANNIE S. SWAN.

Aldersyde, Gullane.

CONTENTS

ILLUSTRATIONS

" This is the true joy of life, the being used for a purpose recognised by yourself as a mighty one ; the being thoroughly worn out before you are thrown on the scrap heap ; the being a force of Nature instead of a feverish, selfish little clod of ailments and grievances ; complaining that the world will not devote itself to making you happy."

GEORGE BERNARD SHAW

CHAPTER ONE

BEGINNINGS

A MONG the numerous factors which have helped to mould me I would rank high the sense of wonder and the capacity to believe almost anything. I am aware that this is a damaging statement with which to preface a serious auto-biography. I can even hear certain critics exclaim, " What a fool the woman must be, to give herself away at the very outset ! "

Well—perhaps—nevertheless to this dual force I attribute a considerable measure of such success as I have achieved.

A supreme and immovable faith in the inherent and ultimate soundness and goodness of human nature is, I admit, somewhat difficult, if not to acquire, at least to preserve. Those in whom it is inborn should thank God, fasting. Possessing such a talisman, life may batter, but it will never defeat them.

This faith—God its origin—has survived in me every assault of Fate.

The sense of wonder is, of course, the heritage of every child. In some, however, it is early shattered, quite frequently by others. He enters the world with eyes and ears open to receive every impression it has to offer. He will never be disappointed in the feast the Creator has spread for him, but his contact with human beings may, and alas ! often does, destroy its pristine glory.

I can remember quite acutely the passionate, almost ecstatic joy I experienced, when very small, beholding the wonder and the beauty of earth and sea and sky. Sunset and sunrise, the still dawn and the evening hush ; the dew on the grass shimmering in the sun, filling the cups of the daisies and the primroses on the bank ; the sudden, swift flight of a bird, the joyous trill of " the laverock in the lift "—I cannot recall a time when these did not thrill.

Nevertheless, my first conscious memory is not of anything so exquisite, but of my first lie. It was a quite deliberate lie, conceived and carried into execution when I was, I should imagine, about five. I not only told it myself, but basely tempted two infant brothers to share my crime. Its origin, of course, was fear, the cause of many deviations from the truth.

It happened at the farm of Temple Hall, in Berwickshire, near the village of Coldingham, which my father, in his hunger for land, had acquired on a lease. It proved one of the failures of his life. The occasion was either harvest or haymaking-time, for they were building stacks in the farmyard. A good-natured ploughman allowed us to be on the top of the stack with him, while he received and stamped in the sheaves. It was a glorious ploy for youngsters, and we threw ourselves into it with all our might. It was a warm summer's day, and growing hot with exertion, I threw off my hat, a brand-new one, with a gay blue ribbon tied about the crown. When the time came to descend the ladder, the hat was nowhere to be found, having been covered up and tramped on, doubtless, under the sheaves. As we toddled back to the house, minus the hat, I conceived the base scheme of asserting, with blandly innocent air, that I had not had the hat on, and therefore could not know where it was. I can't remember whether that shady explanation was accepted—but the memory of the lie remains.

It was my father we stood in awe of, never my mother. He had a high and passionate temper, a very stern mien, and though he never thrashed us, could strike terror into our souls. Even after I had a house of my own, I instinctively rose when he entered the room. His personality demanded obeisance rather than affection. In the light of maturer knowledge and experience, I now realise that much of that sternness was assumed to hide his real nature. He was afraid of himself. Many Scots of the old school were like that, hence the strange bleakness of much of the family life.

My mother was entirely different, so gentle, so even, so wonderful in every way that, when we who are left compare notes, we cannot recall ever having seen her ruffled. She was one of the most

reserved and silent women I have ever met. She
passed from us before we even knew her. She was
a born home-maker, a past mistress in the art of
creating beauty and utility out of the most slender
and unpromising of materials. She never had a
penny of her own ; nor had any encouragement to
spend, even when money was not scarce, but she
never grumbled, nor showed either impatience or
irritation. Knowing now how much she had to
bear, my one regret is that she did not live long
enough for her numerous brood to sweeten and
enrich her later years.

My father was a son of the soil, and his passion
for it was his undoing. Although he had a perfectly good business as a potato merchant, he could
not keep away from the land. It was a highly
speculative business, buying the potato crop in the
field, and trusting to a profit when it was turned
over in the market. But it suited his temperament.
He passed on a bit of that speculative flair to me,
for I have never been afraid to take risks nor to
plunge into new adventures, even when they did
not present a very promising development. He
had a very high standing in the markets. One who
had done much business with him told me that
" Edward Swan would divide a ha'penny in the
cause of justice."

When the Berwickshire venture failed, we moved
to Edinburgh, where he continued the business of
buying and selling potatoes. Some of my happiest
memories are centred in the old house of Maryfield,

which stood at the head of the Easter Road, then a lovely country lane, bordered by fields and hedges, white with may bloom, and pink wild roses in summer. Maryfield was an old family mansion, with a beautiful garden and excellent stabling. It was an ideal home for a family of seven " steerin' bairns," and we enjoyed the life, in company with a regular Zoo, consisting of a pony, a goat, dogs and cats, and hens.

My father was very anxious to buy the property, but, owing to some flaw in the title-deeds necessitating the consent of a shareholder in the estate, who could not be found, the sale could not then be effected. It was a pity, for it would have been a rich, gilt-edged investment, the whole of that district having become a teeming industrial area, every square foot of great value.

The old house has long disappeared, but often, dashing past that corner in the car, I see through misted eyes that happy band of children, wild and full of mischief. There was a great chestnut tree in the corner of the garden. We used to climb up into its branches, from which, safely hidden, we dropped pebbles and things on passers-by. Top hats, or " lum hats," as they were called, were our chief aversion and made acceptable targets.

Our grandmother lived with us then, a rather terrible, but very clever, old woman, whose temper was so outrageous that neither of her married daughters would shelter her. My mother, angel that she was, put up with her without a murmur.

2

When in one of her tantrums, she would lock herself in her room, and her meals, set out on a tray, had to be left on the mat outside. Of course she should have been left till hunger drove her forth, but my mother was incapable of indulging in any form of retaliation.

For some strange reason, I was my grandmother's favourite. She constantly predicted a brilliant future for a plain and tiresome child.

She died soon after we left Maryfield, of a broken heart, I believe, because she so hated the little house into which we had moved. Her contempt for it was unbounded. We all hated it, and it was a joy day when we heard that our father had acquired another farm, near Gorebridge, Midlothian.

His ideal life was the country in summer and the warm and cheerful town in winter. For a time, while things were going well, he achieved that ideal. We were all at school then, and only went out to Mountskip for the holidays.

We attended a Dame's school kept by a very remarkable, brilliant woman called Miss Jane Stage. Never was there a more able or thorough instructress, and I owe my knowledge of grammar and general proficiency in the English language entirely to the grounding received in that modest establishment in Haddington Place. From there I passed on to the Queen Street Ladies' College (one of the most distinguished of the Merchant Company's schools) to acquire a few frills. I am bound to confess that, entirely through my own fault, I learned very little there. I had been accustomed at the Dame's school to individual attention instead of large classes and teaching in the mass. I made no use of what I now recognise was a great opportunity, and because I failed to win a bursary or a scholarship, was removed at an earlier age than is common nowadays. I still have a warm side to the school, however, and am always glad when I can attend any of their functions. It gave me quite a thrill when I went, not long ago, to address both the big school and the little school, remembering the furtive, shrinking creature of sixty years ago.

The Church was a very important factor in our life at that time. My father, in his youth, had come under the influence of the Morisonian revival, which was a revolt against the harsh and narrow Calvinistic doctrines. Free grace for every man, and pardon for all repentant sinners, was the essence of his creed ; and anything in the shape of election or pre-ordination was to him in the nature of a red rag to a bull.

While we were at Maryfield, he attached himself to the little Evangelical Union Church at Leith, and our Sunday morning walk was down the sweet country lane now called Easter Road. He helped to build that little church, was one of its office-bearers, and loved it with every fibre of his being. It is still a live and progressive congregation, carrying out the old traditions laid down by its saintly founders.

Our social life was all bound up in that little

church, our friends were there, and we loved everything connected with it. It was a great wrench for all of us when my father discovered that an absentee farmer cannot farm successfully, and decreed that we must go out to Mountskip and make a permanent home. This necessitated the younger children, two brothers and two sisters, travelling by train to Edinburgh every day, and it was my job to drive them to and from the station, a distance of two and a half miles. In winter we had to start in pitch darkness to catch the eight o'clock train. We had great winters then, almost arctic in their severity. The drifted snow was quite often level with the hedges, and a single track cut through it by the snow plough. We used to run along the frozen tops of the hedges, trying to touch the telegraph wires. I think we had warmer summers, however. I seem to remember long golden days of intense heat.

It was, on the whole, a pleasant family life. A houseful of boys and girls, sturdy and healthy, can't be kept in continuous subjection. They have ways of escape, in irrepressible spirits, complete lack of responsibility, and general dare-devil courage. We had all those in full measure, pressed down and running over. Our father had a wide range of slogans for the direction of youth:

" Them that winna work shouldna eat."

" Young folk should never be tired."

" Early to bed, early to rise."

" Less noise, see, or clear out ! "

These could be multiplied *ad infinitum*. But I do not think, in spite of his tremendous energy, that he was himself a hard worker. He must have been, in his youth, judging from the tales he told us, but I remember him as a driving force, intent on getting the best out of everybody. He did not always succeed, for there was nothing persuasive or encouraging about him.

Work was his fetish. From him I acquired the capacity for work and reverence for it, which has been my strong suit all the years of my active life. To this day I can't bear to waste a minute, and the delicate abandon of leisure has been a sealed book to me. It is a proof that, however hard we try, we do not, and cannot, get away from our early environment.

From him also I acquired a certain restlessness of spirit which has pursued me unceasingly. He was always reaching out after some new experience, something that was going to better him, and be more worth while than anything yet attempted.

My mother ? Did I then learn nothing from her ? Yes, a passionate love for beauty in humanity, in nature—in literature and art. She was very partially educated, but hers was by far the finer nature of that queerly assorted pair. I remember finding her at the baking-board one day, with an open book turned face downwards on the table. I lifted it eagerly to see what was powerful enough to so engage her attention. It was Cowper's *Task*, a book then far beyond my comprehension or

interest.   I have often thought of all that must have
been repressed and hidden in that still nature, of
what she had to suffer from us all, and her endless
patience.   But I am sure she had compensations.
I have seen her standing on the doorstep, looking
away across the wide landscape to the sea, with an
expression of still rapture on her face.   When
spoken to, it was as if she came back with a startled
air from some region beyond, lovely and desirable,
to the stark reality of daily living.

She, too, was a tireless worker in household ways
—baking, cooking, washing, mending, and making.
Never did any of us see those hands folded in quiet
rest, till the end came.   She was a marvellous
contriver in a shabby house, and no mean carpenter.
If she had had money to spend or to burn, I can
imagine her in a riot of beauty and of colour.

Once she surprised us all by retiring to her room
for a whole day, abandoning everything.   The
mystery was explained by a copy of *East Lynne*,
which had been brought surreptitiously into the
house, and in which she became so engrossed that
she ceased to " care a hang," as we expressed it, for
anything or anybody.   I am sure she would have
been one of my keenest critics, and her sense of
humour, which, though repressed, quite often
bubbled forth, would have been very excellent for
any budding authoress.

Soon after we went to live at Mountskip, my
eldest sister, Phemie, was married to the son of a
family we had known well in Edinburgh.   We had

a pretty country wedding, people arriving in gigs
and carriages, the ceremony in the upstairs parlour,
and a large, solid luncheon table set out in the living-
room.

I remember the consternation in my soul when I
saw my father, after the young couple had disappeared down the drive, dashing round by the
garden wall with the tears streaming down his
cheeks. She was the first of that bright band to
leave the parental nest. Now, alas !—

> " Their graves are scattered far and wide,
>   O'er mount, and stream, and sea."

CHAPTER TWO

THE FAMILY

THERE was nothing abnormal or striking about our family life. Quite frequently we " cast out " with one another, quarrelling at work and at play. But, as a family, we had few serious differences, and to-day the clan feeling is as strong as ever in the remnant that is left.

There were, however, some features in that queer little grey farmhouse which set it apart from others in the same class. We shared everything—our love of the " brute beasts," as my father called them, all the seasonal joys of the farm, the adventures which healthy children can find in the world of make-believe, especially when there is unlimited space to roam in, woods and fields to be explored, burns to fish, unlawful and forbidden territories to be raided, with a fearful, perilous joy. But our chief passion, regarding which in that family of seven there was not one rebel or dissentient voice, was the passion for books.

We had very few—possibly the reason why our hunger, always unappeased, was frequently acute. Against the wall in the living-room stood a rather beautiful old Chippendale bookcase of genuine merit, which our heathen taste, alas! failed to appreciate. I am afraid that was our attitude towards all the old stuff in the farmhouse, since a lovely old sideboard of quite authentic value was allowed to be sold for six shillings at a " roup " which occurred later. It found a home in a neighbouring dairy, where the milk pans were plumped down on it, marring its exquisite surface. Ignorance, what crimes are committed in thy name !

The principal item in the bookcase was eighteen volumes of the *Penny Encyclopædia*, which had been left as a legacy to my father by an old uncle, who had been a tutor in " noble families," and had acquired a small library of his own. It was a mine of wealth to us, and especially to me. I spent hours poring over it, gloating specially over the weird and highly coloured diagrams of sections of the human body. It may have been coming events casting their shadows before, though after I was married to a doctor I never opened a medical book. The effect of the *Encyclopædia* on a vivid imagination was to give me all the diseases therein described. I suffered agonies from them, quite frequently arranged and attended my own funeral, and was generally a complete blight and nuisance to myself and everybody else. How my relations didn't murder me, I can't think. They had plenty of provocation. They must have been a long-suffering lot.

There were a few other books, but little or no

fiction. My father's pet masterpiece was Jane Porter's *Scottish Chiefs*, of which he believed every word. That was his attitude to the Bible, too. He believed that every line was inspired and was the true Word of God. At family worship he read the Bible from cover to cover, not missing out the Levitical law or the chapters consisting entirely of the names of the tribesmen. " So-and-So begat somebody else ! " We used to fall sound asleep, getting up automatically when it was time to kneel down for the prayer, when we fell asleep again. But every word of that prayer I remember to this day. It never varied, and was a most comprehensive and well-put-together account of personal and family needs.

The reverential voice, breathing assurance that a Heavenly Father was listening to every word, left an impression on my mind which remains to this day. If it was not a faith that could move mountains, at least it was a shield and stand-by in the day of trouble, or when times were hard. And that was their normal state. When through excessive rains corn was growing green in the stooks or potatoes rotting in the furrows, there never was a word of complaint. Gloom, of course, but because it was the will of God that the wind should blow and the floods descend, poor earthly worms must simply bow the reverential knee.

It was a wonderful way to live, and I submit that no philosopher, scientist, or plain materialist has ever been able to present a satisfying substitute.

You did your best, and left the rest. It has been the solution of many a problem in my life.

There were some bound volumes of sound magazines, such as *Good Words, Chambers*, and the *Sunday Magazine*. Then, to crown all, there was Shakespeare !

The first Shakespeare Society I ever heard of was in our own home at Mountskip. The members consisted of the whole family, except my mother, who, sitting in the chimney corner with the work from which her hands never rested, composed the audience. We had a parrot, who sometimes interpolated a remark here and there, on occasion singularly appropriate. It was a weird bird, a great pet of my father's. It would follow him about everywhere, and when it escaped—which was quite often—would come down from the highest tree at his bidding. We used to act the plays, without scenery or equipment, of course. It was actually a reading circle, with the parts in the plays apportioned as seemed most fit. I see my father now as Shylock, standing at the table, declaiming at the top of his voice. I can't remember about Portia or the others. His personality and voice in my memory dominate the scene.

While all this was going on, I was aware of creative stirrings in my mind and heart. I had always been a first-class story-teller, gathering my schoolfellows about me at odd moments and regaling them chiefly with plagiarised editions of other people's stories. I could always, I imagined, improve them. To satisfy me they must have a happy end—everybody be sorted up, and no loose threads left anywhere. The fiction of that day was highly moral, as well as very limited in its scope. Vice was punished and virtue rewarded as, alas! it seldom is in real life. But one of the functions of imagination is to carry us as far as possible from the realm of reality. Without it, life indeed would be drab, often unendurable.

Our social life, which, associated with our church life, had been very happy in Leith, was very meagre in the country. The farms were isolated, and moreover, my father, in his passion for making other people work, did not approve of diversions of any kind. He discouraged young people about the house because they interrupted the daily and hourly routine. His own hard upbringing—he told us he had earned his own living from the age of seven—partly explained this strange attitude towards youth. As we grew older we defied him, sometimes openly, sometimes in secret. But we certainly had very few of the social advantages open to others of our age and acquaintance.

Nor had we many amusements. A very rare tea or supper party at some neighbour's house, a kirk social or soiree, or a concert or penny reading in the village school comprised the sum-total.

But whatever there was, we enjoyed it up to the hilt. There was nothing blasé about us, quite the reverse. We tramped miles in all kinds of weather to those queer entertainments in the village schools to which we, and all the people we knew, were contributors. There was very little criticism. We were all pleased with what we got and gave. I can remember, however, yawning and wishing the boy had been swept off the " burning deck " before anybody had had time to immortalise him in a very dull poem, which appeared on every programme and was recited with more or less—mostly less—dramatic effect.

As no church or chapel in our neighbourhood preached a gospel free enough to suit my father's evangelical taste, we were driven, as many as the trap would hold, to Dalkeith every Sunday to the little Evangelical Union Chapel in a back street.

I played the organ there for several years, but there was none of the warm, intimate sense of communion we had had in the Duke Street Chapel, the sweet savour of which lingers to this day. When I go back, as I do sometimes, to speak at the Men's Meeting there, I feel as if I " belonged " in a sense I have never felt in any other church. I am aware of unseen presence, of something like the flutter of birds' wings. It is those who have gone " away." They, being dead, yet speak.

Out of all these strange contributory factors meanwhile was growing my creative gift. It was with me day and night, urging me to commit to paper the images, the plots, the odd dramas of life and love which chased one another perpetually through an over-active brain. I began modestly with children's stories, and was very fortunate in selling one or two to Blackie & Sons for small sums, ranging from three to five pounds. The money was, of course, very acceptable to an entirely penniless creature, but I can truly say that to gain money has never been the main factor in my writing life. I shall have a good deal to say about this in a later chapter. But it seems necessary to explain about the beginning of things.

The most exciting adventure in these early days was winning a prize in a Christmas Story Competition in the *People's Journal*. John Leng & Company of Dundee were undoubtedly the pioneers in a number of journalistic enterprises, and Scotland owes them a great deal. The *People's Journal* and the *People's Friend* both came into our house every week, and were devoured from cover to cover. I tried my luck at the Christmas Story Competition and was successful in winning the second prize with a story entitled " Tom Arnold : A Brief Autobiography." It contained material sufficient for a quite respectable novel. Experience taught me later to be a little less prodigal in use of my raw material.

Tremendous was the excitement on that wild and snowy Saturday morning when I returned with the gig, plus the family post-bag *and* the *Journal*, containing the news of my success. The prize was three pounds, which I exuberantly burst on Christmas presents.

It was a direct encouragement to persevere, and laid the foundations of my long and happy connection, through a whole lifetime, with the Dundee firm.

My parents regarded all these efforts with an odd kind of tolerant amusement, but my writing had to be done largely in secret and in holes and corners. For really we had very little leisure in our working day. It began in the morning at five o'clock in summer and six in winter. There were no servants in the house and the work was apportioned among us. There were fires to be lit, breakfast to get, cows to be milked, then in general sequence the cooking, baking, washing, and mending for the whole family. There were also outdoor workers to be fed in the kitchen at stated intervals. There were three of us, my mother, my sister Janet, and myself.

My younger sister Mary entered the teaching profession and became a pupil teacher at the village school, which enabled her to live at home till she went to college. That was the old system. All is changed now.

In winter we had long evenings, but I can remember often being too tired to work, or even to think. We had no modern conveniences, not even water in the house. We had to carry it in buckets from the pump, or when the pump was frozen, from a well a good way off. There were also coals to be carried in, lamps trimmed, and all sorts of really hard work about which the modern housewife knows but little.

My father had at first no use at all for my wasting

time trying to write. Although he loved books, he could not conceive that any child of his might have the ambition or the capacity to write one. His attitude towards the writing fraternity was like that of an old Borderer, an uncle of Tom Scott, R.S.A., who, meeting his nephew in Selkirk one day, after he had decided to take up an artist's career, said :

" I suppose you'd rather do that than *work* ? " Terrific emphasis on the " work."

Tom Scott told us that tale with great gusto when he came out to Gorebridge to make the sketches for *Carlowrie.* Authorship was not then, in certain circles, at least, considered a very respectable occupation. Apparently art was also looked upon askance.

On the whole we had a very jolly youth. Sex questions were never discussed. It was the day when everything was decently covered up. We were all, however, quite aware of the problems of adolescence and also of the sordid side of village and farm life. We didn't talk about any of it, however, and four girls married in complete ignorance of the physical side of matrimony.

Nothing happened to us in consequence. We were able to " warstle through," and make, in most cases, a better job of it than many of the over-sexed and highly initiated to-day. We took it in our stride, so to speak. Who shall say it was not the sensible way ?

CHAPTER THREE

MANY CHANGES

I CHERISHED many wild though secret ambitions in these early days, and, I fear, gave myself some airs in consequence. I determined to become a real author, whom the public would consider seriously and whose name would appear frequently in the papers. Above all, I was determined to get to London, the Mecca of so many literary and other dreams. I had not the faintest idea how this was going to be accomplished, but I never had any doubt about that section of my dreams coming true.

I worked steadily on, stealing, I fear, a good deal of the time which was supposed to be devoted to household tasks, receiving countless rebuffs ; one small manuscript returning to me a dozen times. I don't know whether that particular one ultimately found a home, probably not. I must have been blessed with a large share of my father's incurable optimism, for I never got really discouraged. The joy was in the work, not in any possible reward. It is so to this day.

So little practical knowledge had I of the pub-

3

lishing world that I quite often sent my stuff to firms long since defunct, getting the addresses from the title-pages of ancient tomes in our limited book-case. I was absolutely without literary advice of any kind, but I don't think it was a serious depriva-tion. I went through the mill alone, and in the end profited by sad experience.

When I acquired some standing in the world of books, my work was enormously added to by requests for advice, which usually entailed the perusal of bulky manuscripts. I have in my time done an enormous amount of this kind of work, and am convinced now that it was, in the great majority of cases, not only a thankless task but a sheer waste of time. The only kind of advice the usual brand of budding author wants is praise. But of this more anon. I feel sure it is better to fight one's way upward or onward unaided.

My first novel, a very crude effort called *Ups and Downs*, was published in London by an obscure, and possibly rather shady, firm called The Charing Cross Publishing Company, which later came to grief in the law courts. They advertised largely in obscure papers, where they were more likely to catch the unwary. They published on the half-profit system and had a grandiloquent system of correspondence which did not fail to impress an ignoramus like myself, who did not know that reputable publishing houses do not need to advertise themselves, their reputation being wide enough to reach all they wish to reach. Advertising for MSS.

suitable for publication was quite unknown among them.

I sent my story to The Charing Cross Publishing Company, and after they had considered it, they offered to publish it on the half-profit system, my share in the cost of production being something over fifty pounds. Being quite penniless, I showed the correspondence to my father who, aware that I had already earned a few guineas by my pen, thought there might be something in writing after all. He agreed to advance the money.

The whole affair was a ghastly failure, though the book had several quite good reviews, notably one in the *Athenæum*, then reckoned a high authority in the literary and critical world.

My father was very angry at losing his money, and I had to keep very quiet about my literary efforts or ambitions for a long time. I don't remember feeling oppressed by the debt, and never offered to pay it back. In later years I had ample opportunities of acknowledging it.

The urge to write, however, continued unabated. For several years I contributed all sorts of stuff to the *Christian Leader*, a very up-to-date religious and literary paper founded by the late Rev. Howie Wylie, one of the most accomplished litterateurs I have ever met. Under his editorship the *Leader* was a force, but it could not survive without him.

So far as I was concerned, the work was a labour **of love.** All the payment I ever got was an IOU

for fifteen pounds, which I discovered years after
among some old papers. But in spite of that, I
feel that the debt remains on my side, not on his.
He gave me the chance to express myself, and a lot
of wise and valuable counsel besides. He believed
in me, and that meant a great deal to one struggling
against discouragement at home.

I had at this time a rather curious literary adventure ; if literary it could be called. The proprietor of a Lancashire evening paper, who had come
in contact with some of my printed effusions, wrote
asking whether I would contribute a story of
religious and domestic nature to his paper at a
fixed salary of one pound per week. It was an
extraordinary proposal and meant colossal output,
but I was not earning anything at the time, so I
accepted. Later, I was invited to come to Oldham
and see the place and the people for whom I was
catering. This man, fanatically pious—I can't
really call him religious—had started the paper to
combat the sinister influence of the daily press.
No betting or gambling news was permitted in
the paper, and police reports were strictly supervised
and censored.

I have very shadowy memories of that strange
visit to Oldham. I have even forgotten the names
of the people who entertained me in a lordly mansion,
the like of which I had never seen. My taste,
perhaps, was a bit crude and countrified, but I
could not admire a woman who wore three large
gold brooches pinned on to her bodice in the morning.

One was a large coloured picture, possibly a miniature of her lord and master.

I was taken to see the factories, and remember being thrilled at the endless streams of mill-workers pouring through the gates—my potential public !

I went home and wrote the story he wanted, but it was not approved by my employer. I made the fatal mistake of choosing my heroine from the working-class and allowing her master's son to fall in love with her. It was pointed out to me at great length and with much unction what a pernicious effect this sort of stuff might have on the young women who would read it. He printed the story, with copious alterations carried out by himself. I got the money for it, but our connection came to an end. It could not have lasted, anyway, as it was frightful work turning out a chapter per day. Later, when I went into the actual figures, it came out at less than a farthing a line. The term " penny-a-liner " was even then applied contemptuously to those who were obliged to earn their living by their pen and accepted what they could get. My farthing-a-line fiction put me on even a lower scale.

All the while I was working secretly for about two years on *Aldersyde*. Having no money to spend on good stationery, I wrote the first copy on the blank pages of a discarded ledger of my father's, hiding it all in a box in the little wardrobe room, off the upstairs parlour. I covered the box with a bit of odd stuff, so that it looked like a stool. There my secret was safe.

My writing—indeed all our activities—suffered check by a long term of serious illness in the family, the culminating tragedy of which was our mother's death. The shadows began to close in on the little grey farmhouse hid in the lap of the Lothian hills, never really to lift again.

My brother Alec returned from a visit to the Channel Islands carrying the seeds of typhoid fever. He was violently ill for many weeks, and several of us had mild attacks. Before he was quite convalescent, my mother, worn out with nursing and anxiety, succumbed. She died on the night of the great storm, October 13, 1881, which wrought such havoc on land and sea, destroying the major portion of the Eyemouth fishing fleet. It was a black day for thousands in Scotland.

For us it meant the break up, in fact the end, of the life we had known.

.   .   .   .   .   .

My father married again in little more than a year's time a woman of suitable age, an old friend of the family.

The lot of the stepmother is seldom an easy one. Where there is a large and more or less hostile family to encounter and conciliate, she needs all the sympathy and help she can get. She also needs the wisdom of the serpent and the harmlessness of the dove, allied to a very special grace. There wasn't an earthly chance of our stepmother being a success. To begin with, she had none of the qualities which might have ensured it.

Pious, rigid, narrow-minded, economical to the verge of parsimony, she was the very antithesis of our gentle, generous, charitable mother, who judged nobody and had compassion and loving-kindness for all. She had a dour, determined temper, and in a very short time had my father completely in subjection. The dominator became the dominated. Possibly there was a kind of rough justice in this, but it was pathetic to behold, and I couldn't bear it.

When he would call at my house, after I married, he would say : " Ye needna tell Barbara I've been here."

That sentence revealed a lot. She was intensely jealous of us all, and, of course, was never able to dominate any of us, not even my young sister Margaret, who, in a very little time, was the only one left under the parental roof.

Janet, who had been the housekeeper since our mother's death, left the house before the newly wed came back from their honeymoon. I was engaged to be married and looking forward to a life of my own, and, moreover, possessing the faculty of seeing the other person's point of view. I felt no anger against my father, and even attended the wedding with my fiancé, who acted as groomsman.

This curious detachment of mind is one of the reasons why I could not become an effective politician.

The affection between my father and my husband was very deep and real, more apparent—on the surface, at least—than that between him and his own sons.

The new régime did not last long, so far as the family life was concerned. It was completely disintegrated in a few months. My brothers emigrated to Australia, where the younger one, David, died of pneumonia contracted in their flooded farmhouse. I married my schoolmaster, which meant that he had to sacrifice for the time being his own private dream, which was to study for the medical profession.

But before that happened, *Aldersyde* was completed and published.

The story was frankly modelled on the Border stories of Mrs. Oliphant, for whom I had passionate admiration, amounting to worship. If she had known how devotedly I admired her, I feel sure she would not have made the virulent attack on me she did in the " Old Saloon " in *Blackwood's Magazine.*

I often felt sorry after that I did not write to her at the time, but I was young and shy in those days and stood in great awe of those who had " arrived " in the world of letters. They were to me enchanted figures. She complained in *Blackwood,* after my second book, *Carlowrie,* appeared, that my books went into as many editions as French novels, a most regrettable circumstance since they presented an entirely distorted view of Scottish life and character. I could easily have challenged that, for I wrote almost entirely of the life with which I was familiar, and though the judgment of a young

ANNIE S. SWAN
THE YEAR " ALDERSYDE " WAS PUBLISHED

girl was necessarily immature, the public had no fault to find with it and asked for more. After all, it is the reading public which passes the final judgment on any book. It was as true then as it is to-day, and no amount of log-rolling will launch poor or careless work. It may possibly be launched, but its voyage will be short and its landing disappointing.

I met Mrs. Oliphant in the flesh only once, some years later, in the house of Principal Tulloch at St. Andrews, a gentle, sweet-faced old lady with lovely white hair. I don't know whether she suspected my identity, as I was introduced by my married name. The incident was not mentioned. Anyhow, I should never have had the courage to allude to it. She had a very sad face. I was told it was her habitual expression, and when I read her life, I knew the reason why.

Aldersyde had various adventures before it reached port. It came back from several firms without comment, but at last was accepted by Messrs. Oliphant, Anderson & Ferrier, a very old-established house, just then in need of some new blood infusion. I can never forget the sheer joy of receiving the proof sheets of what I felt sure was to introduce me to the real world of letters. Oliphants promised to produce it handsomely, and Tom Scott, afterwards a well-known R.S.A., was sent out to Yarrow to make sketches for the illustrations.

The book was published in the spring of 1883,

and was immediately reviewed very favourably by
the leading newspapers.

Those were days of palpitating excitement, not
only for me but for all at home. My father began
to smile once more on my endeavours. Each day
there came some fresh thrill—a new review, a kind
letter, something to lift life above the commonplace.

I question if any joy can equal that in a lifetime.
It was the pure essence of spring. All the world,
including me, was young. There are second, even
sometimes third springs, but none have the pristine
glory of the first. Looking back upon it now, I
know it to have been without alloy.

Soon after the publication of *Aldersyde* Mr. Gladstone entered on his famous Midlothian Campaign,
his platform being Irish Home Rule. We all immediately became politicians, for he was a wizard
to whom it was impossible to listen without being
thrilled and converted. I remember running down
to the road end to offer a basket of primroses to him
as he passed. My father, who had no particular
politics, was also impressed to the extent of speaking
very bluntly to the young Earl of Dalkeith, who
was opposing the Campaign, when he came to
solicit his vote on the Tory side. He looked the
young man over and said solemnly : " Man, I've
seen Gladstone. Ye havena an airthly chance."

I was carried away by enthusiasm and went to
Dalkeith to hear him address a mass meeting of
women in the Corn Exchange. That wonderful
speech, with its passionate plea for self-expression

Ap. 16. 83

Dear Madam

I have now read
the work which you did
me the honour to present to
me with a very kind inscription, and I feel obliged to add
a line to my former acknow-
ledgments already sent. I think
it beautiful as a work of art
and it must be the fault of a

reader if he does not profit
by the perusal. Miss Nesbit
and Margt will I hope long
hold their places among the
truly living Sketches of Scottish
character. I remain
dear Madam
Yours very faithful
& obedient,
WEGladstone

Miss Swan

for " little peoples," the silvery voice, the whole magnetism of the man, made an indelible impression on my mind.

I went home and sent him a copy of *Aldersyde*, with a covering letter. I scarcely expected a reply. My surprise was stupendous when I received the wonderful letter transcribed here :

> " 10 DOWNING STREET,
> " WHITEHALL,
> " *Ap.* 16, '83.

" DEAR MADAM,

I have now read the work which you did me the honour to present to me with a very kind inscription, and I feel obliged to add a line to my formal acknowledgment already sent. I think it beautiful as a work of art, and it must be the fault of a reader if he does not profit by the perusal. Miss Nesbit and Marget will, I hope, long hold their places among the truly living sketches of Scottish character.— I remain, dear Madam, your very faithful and obedient,   W. E. GLADSTONE.

" Miss Swan."

I sent it on to the publishers as a kind of reassurance, for they had laid great stress on the risks they took in publishing the work of an unknown person. I cried next morning, when I saw it reproduced in the *Scotsman*, being too young and ignorant to know that Mr. Gladstone had written the letter for that purpose. I felt it so keenly that I wrote to him, explaining and apologising. He was very kind, if rather amused, about it, and sent me several reassuring post cards. He was kind to me in other ways, giving me special admission to the House of Commons on great, epoch-making nights. I was there till morning on the occasion of the Parnell debate.

For the entire copyright of *Aldersyde* I received the sum of fifty pounds, nor was it afterwards supplemented in any way. I shall have something to say in a later chapter about the financial and other rewards of authorship.

I was entirely satisfied with the terms. To a needy person fifty pounds was a great sum. It meant much more to me than that, however.

It was my serious, and, in a small way, triumphant entry into the world of letters.

ALDERSYDE, GULLANE

MOUNTSKIP

CHAPTER FOUR

EDINBURGH IN THE 'EIGHTIES

MY marriage, hastened on by the discomfort and friction at home, took place in 1883. It meant that my husband had to abandon his dream of a medical career. His own home—from which circumstances had already completely estranged him—could offer no help. It was a drastic step we took, on our own initiative and on such slender means as might have daunted the bravest. I was then earning very little, and that little precarious. That is one of the snags, if I may use the expression, of the writing profession. Nothing about it can be certain or secure. Your public even may be here to-day and gone to-morrow. It has all the lure of a game of chance.

We spent the first two years in the little schoolhouse at Star, Markinch, a queer, individual little village where I got the material for two books, *Homespun* and *The Gates of Eden*.

The Gates of Eden was considered by many the best book I had yet produced. I may say that I have had more personal letters about it than about any other. Old men have told me of help and inspiration they got from it in their youth.

It was a queer, restricted life we led in the little Star schoolhouse, and before we had been very long there we began to have dreams of a different future. I have sometimes felt in myself an odd power of projecting myself into the future. I felt sure I was going to succeed as a writer, and that such success must mean a wider sphere and different surroundings from the little schoolhouse on the edge of Star Moss. Obviously the husband I loved must not lag behind.

So we began to talk of the possibility of his resuming his medical studies. We had saved quite a little bit, there being no temptation to spend there, so we decided to take the plunge. I don't remember that we asked anybody's advice. In the big things of life decisions have to be taken alone. I have in my time, by request, given much advice, but I can't honestly say that I have ever had any faith in its effects. People generally have their minds made up before they seek advice. All they want is confirmation.

To our surprise and mild dismay, we found that the whole family, plus a lot of busybodies who had no right to interfere, actively disapproved of the step we proposed to take. All our connections made haste to assure us that neither sympathy nor help would be received from them.

Fortunately we had not counted on it, so it didn't matter much. We had privately canvassed and considered the whole position and prospects, and were prepared, we fully believed, for all the difficulties lying ahead. They far exceeded even the dismal prophecies of friends and relations, but as we kept our mouths shut nobody knew how near the wind we sailed during those testing years. Quite often we had not enough to eat.

But they were great years on which we afterwards looked back with a kind of wistful regret. Everybody should have a taste of poverty at some time or other. It is an educative and purifying experience, when not unduly prolonged, so that the iron enters into the soul.

We went through to Mountskip to acquaint my father with our decision, and he was horrified. He could not grasp our point of view at all, nor understand why anybody should wish to leave a secure position, where there was enough to live on in modest comfort, for what seemed to him " perfect nonsense." Those were the words he used. I remember them well. He did not say very much to Jim, but talking to me privately inquired whether I realised that for a few years the burden of the livelihood must rest chiefly on me. It was a preposterous idea to one who regarded woman as the weaker vessel, totally dependent by divine ordination, in every capacity, on the nobler male.

But we stuck to our guns. When is youth ever really daunted either by hazard or danger ? We live too softly these days, and they say that youth is afraid of risks. We just laughed at them, and laugh would roll out, while his dark eyes fairly danced with glee.   Here is a sample :

A man in Kirkconnel who had a small painter's and decorator's business was commissioned to do some outside painting at a neighbour's house.   Not being very clear about the details, he repaired to the house early one morning and was met by drawn blinds and a tearful wife at the door.   The Scotchman's strong line about emotion is to ignore it, so he merely inquired whether he could see John. When informed that John had passed away in the night, he gave his shoulders a hitch and said inquiringly :

" Ay, ay—imphm—he widna say onything aboot green pent ? "

It seems to me, looking back, that Edinburgh in the 'eighties was a very interesting city, with a more distinctive flavour than it possesses to-day.

There was a small select company, if not of the immortals, at least of rare souls, who did much to clarify and sweeten the air.   The most outstanding one was Dr. John Brown, the author of *Rab and his Friends*.   I never met him, but I had seen the old man, with the benevolent, saintly face, taking the air in the vicinity of his home.

We knew the Patrick Geddeses well, and were frequent guests at the weird but delightful parties they gave in their flat in the Lawnmarket.   They were certainly pioneers in welfare work, their idea being that the only way to bring light and sweetness to slum dwellers was to go and live among them.

It was a noble experiment, which bore much fruit in after-days.

I remember going to see the late Mrs. Anna Geddes one winter afternoon to find her in a little underground schoolroom, teaching tiny tots, not yet of school age, who would otherwise have been playing in the gutter. Her graceful figure in a green gown, her sweet, smiling face, lightened the shadows in that queer place. When their own children came, they had to remove their habitation to more salubrious surroundings.

There were two women writers in Edinburgh then whom I knew intimately. Mrs. Jessie Saxby, who had made a reputation by her songs and stories of the Shetland Isles, of which she was a native. She lived in a dear, quaint little house on a slope facing Samson's Ribs, in the Queen's Park. She had a unique and striking personality, very clever and charming. There was true Scandinavian fire in her eyes when denouncing wrongs or injustices. She afterwards returned to Shetland, and is alive still. She must be nearly a centenarian by now. I got into touch with her again, after a lapse of half a century, through a casual paragraph in a newspaper.

The other was Robina Hardy, a very different woman, couthy, kind, and genial. She leaped into local fame with a story of the Grassmarket slums called *Jock Halliday*. She was a delightful creature, full of wit and kindly humanity. It did you good even to look at her. She gave afternoon parties at little to do with the intellect, and is either lost or won through the affections."

We remained two and a half years in Edinburgh, then, being a little better off, moved to a house on the sea front at Musselburgh. I don't know why we did that, for it was certainly less convenient for University classes and everything else.

It seemed to be our doom to march on. We might indeed, as the years rolled by, have had engraved on the lintels of our ever-changing doors—

"A rolling stone gathers no moss."

It was a noble experiment, which bore much fruit in after-days.

I remember going to see the late Mrs. Anna Geddes one winter afternoon to find her in a little underground schoolroom, teaching tiny tots, not yet of school age, who would otherwise have been playing in the gutter. Her graceful figure in a green gown, her sweet, smiling face, lightened the shadows in that queer place. When their own children came, they had to remove their habitation to more salubrious surroundings.

There were two women writers in Edinburgh then whom I knew intimately. Mrs. Jessie Saxby, who had made a reputation by her songs and stories of the Shetland Isles, of which she was a native. She lived in a dear, quaint little house on a slope facing Samson's Ribs, in the Queen's Park. She had a unique and striking personality, very clever and charming. There was true Scandinavian fire in her eyes when denouncing wrongs or injustices. She afterwards returned to Shetland, and is alive still. She must be nearly a centenarian by now. I got into touch with her again, after a lapse of half a century, through a casual paragraph in a newspaper.

The other was Robina Hardy, a very different woman, couthy, kind, and genial. She leaped into local fame with a story of the Grassmarket slums called *Jock Halliday*. She was a delightful creature, full of wit and kindly humanity. It did you good even to look at her. She gave afternoon parties at

the old family house in Minto Street, when her sister, who looked exactly as if she had stepped out of an old miniature, used to entertain the company with selections of Scotch airs on the pianoforte. There were no gramophones or mechanical music in those days, and we all listened politely to one another's performances.

There was an exceptional number of bright, clever, interesting women in Edinburgh about that time, with all of whom I had some contact. Feminists were strong too. Mrs. Priscilla Bright Maclaren, sister of John Bright, was the leading spirit along with Miss Wigham, a beautiful, demure little Quakeress, who wore the becoming Quaker dress. Though so sweet and even shrinking in her manner, she was an ardent Feminist, and did her best to get me enrolled as a member of the little band working for " votes for women." It was a very dignified and harmless sort of campaign, completely devoid of violent tactics, but no doubt it did good work, blazing the trail for the more vigorous spirits who came after. I never joined the group ; I had other things to do.

The two Miss Stevensons were prominent in all educational matters, and Miss Flora was the first woman to achieve the chairmanship of the School Board.

But some of my happiest and most grateful memories circle round the house of the Flints in Craigmillar Park. Professor Flint was one of the most distinguished theologians and scholars of his

day. He lived with a devoted sister in a beautiful house on the outskirts, and they were extraordinarily kind to us. They entertained largely; every distinguished visitor to Edinburgh found his or her way to that hospitable house. They never left us out. At their luncheon or dinner table we met wonderful people, among them Oliver Wendell Holmes.

The kindness of the Flints to us was the more conspicuous, because we were so poor and unable to make them any sort of return. I shall never forget the joy we had in London, when we were able to entertain them, and introduce them to some of our distinguished friends. Their joy was quite equal to ours.

I was specially grateful to them in Edinburgh because they were always so attentive to my husband, appearing to realise, with that fine and delicate perception only found in rare souls, the difficulties of his position and the disadvantage attached to it.

Professor Flint had a giant's intellect but the heart of a child. When I took my first child to see him, he kissed and blessed her, and I tried to tell him how often his beneficence had blessed and comforted her father and mother. While I was writing *Maitland of Laurieston*, I ventured to ask him concerning some of the religious problems dealt with in the story. He very kindly overlooked part of the manuscript and returned it without criticism, only this comment : " Remember that religion has

little to do with the intellect, and is either lost or
won through the affections."

We remained two and a half years in Edinburgh,
then, being a little better off, moved to a house on
the sea front at Musselburgh. I don't know why we
did that, for it was certainly less convenient for
University classes and everything else.

It seemed to be our doom to march on. We
might indeed, as the years rolled by, have had
engraved on the lintels of our ever-changing doors—

"A rolling stone gathers no moss."

CHAPTER FIVE

MUSSELBURGH DAYS

MUSSELBURGH had some literary associations. In an old house in the High Street, David Macbeth Moir wrote *Mansie Wauch* under the pseudonym of " Delta." In my book *Maitland of Laurieston*, written in Musselburgh, I ventured to introduce as a minor character the beloved doctor, and I was surprised to hear that his grandson, carrying on the practice in the familiar house, thought I had taken an unwarrantable liberty. It is always dangerous to introduce real people into fiction, however carefully and tenderly it may be done. Nowadays every novel contains the assurance on the fly-leaf that no living person is portrayed therein.

Mrs. Oliphant, then a star in the literary firmament, was born at Wallyford, not far from Musselburgh, but the old farmhouse about which she wrote so tenderly had disappeared and there was nothing interesting or picturesque about the modern one. The scenery and associations, however, could not be destroyed, and in my walks I often used to picture her a happy little girl, before the sorrows of life overtook her, running wild on the uplands or watching the white wings of the sailing boats on the Firth.

Loretto School was then, as now, a feature of Musselburgh life. Hely Almond, that original creative genius and very able man, was Head Master, and the boys in their red stockings and blazers certainly brightened the landscape, as they do now. We used to pity them on cold, wild days in their scanty attire, and wonder whether the result would be the survival of the fittest.

At Musselburgh, besides my regular work for the *People's Friend*, I wrote two books, *Maitland of Laurieston* and *Sheila*. My sister Janet was living with us then, and we were able to afford a good maid, so I had abundance of time for writing. But, with the contrariety of the human mind, I often regretted the strenuous but cosy life in the little flat.

I was fortunate in securing my only entrance to the august pages of *Blackwood* with an article on " The Country Town," about which Mr. Wm. Blackwood wrote me a very kind letter.

We twice spent the long college recess in the schoolhouse at Amulree. My husband was a keen fisherman, and the Braan, also the little lochs, carefully preserved, but sometimes available for a day's fishing, afforded splendid sport. I wrote part of *Sheila* up there, where the scene is laid. Many legends have grown up there round my name. One day, years after, I was driving with some Perth friends to picnic at Amulree. We drove by way of Crieff and the Sma' Glen, and I sat in the driver's seat. He entertained me with many weird tales about myself, not knowing my identity which, of course, I did not reveal.

" Ay, thonder's the wee tree she planted on the hill, an' she wrote the book sittin' on the seat ootside the schoolhouse door." " I never saw her mysel', but I ken folk that did," and so on.

The schoolmaster's sister, who " did " for us at the schoolhouse, told me a very touching incident.

One day one of the wandering folk, selling trifles of lace and such-like in a basket, called at the schoolhouse door, asking to be directed to the house of Dalmore, which was the name I had given to the habitation which some of my characters in *Sheila* occupied. Miss Richardson explained that there was no such house, upon which the inquirer triumphantly produced some newspaper cuttings from her basket with the name Dalmore prominently displayed. When it was explained to her that it was only a story about imaginary people, she turned sadly away, saying it " wasna fair," for she had travelled a long way, sure that the kind lady at Dalmore would purchase her entire stock.

She was so completely disillusioned that I fear, in consequence, I had one reader the less.

The first summer we were there I had the happiness to meet the Dowager Duchess of Atholl, who showed me much kindness in later years. One day, on the moor opposite the schoolhouse, two ladies were sitting on camp-stools, sketching. It came on a wild and terrific thunderstorm, with a deluge of rain, so suddenly that there was no time to escape to the inn. We ran out and begged them to come and shelter, which they did. We had no idea at all who they were, and they talked delightfully, accepted the tea I offered, and when it cleared, went away, thanking us warmly.

A few days later we received an invitation to lunch at The Cottage, Dunkeld, then the residence of the Dowager Duchess of Atholl, grandmother of the present Duke. We were quite thrilled by it. Everything in the way of experience was welcome and valuable to me. We walked the eleven miles to Dunkeld—nothing to us in those days—and had a most enjoyable hour with the Duchess and her cousin, Miss Murray Macgregor. The only guests that day, besides ourselves, was Jane Evans, the last of the Eton dames, who was so beloved by the many distinguished men who passed through her house. Those gentlewomen of the old school were a remarkable trio. There are none like them now. Their grace, their dignity, their knowledge, their exquisite humour, combined to set them apart from ordinary folk.

That visit was not only a revelation to me, it was the beginning of a long friendship with the Duchess. She took the greatest interest in my work and also in our family life, and when she went to London for part of the season, came to see us in our London house.

She must have been very beautiful in her youth, and at eighty held her figure as straightly as a young sapling. I have seen her stand a couple of hours at a Court function with no sign of fatigue or boredom. She was spartanly reared, spending hours on the backboard to ensure a straight back. She told me that she was fifteen years old before she knew there was anything people *could* have for breakfast except porridge. She was very reticent about her long connection with Queen Victoria. Never was the Victorian tradition more rigidly upheld. I felt mildly rebuked one day when, happening to remark on her long association with the Queen, she replied stiffly : " I have had the honour to be her humble servant all my life."

I sometimes think it well that she passed over before all the veils were torn away from great personages, and books written about them without reserve, and not always with good taste. They would undoubtedly have caused her acute indignation and distress.

She offered to present me at Court, which was a great event for me. Always avid for new experience, I was thrilled about it. One day, lunching with her at Eton Place, I inquired whether it was necessary to take lessons in " deportment," as I saw such advertised in *The Times*. She was much amused.

" My dear," she said, " what you have to remember is that the whole object of the Court is to get you through as quickly as possible. Nobody will be aware of what you wear, what you look like, or what you do—unless you make some *faux pas*."

The Victorian Drawing-Room was an appalling function, though nobody dared so much as whisper it then. Buckingham Palace was uninhabited except when the Queen came up, always reluctantly, to hold two, on rare occasions three, Courts during the season. I attended for the first time a March one, in bitter weather.

I must not forget to say that it was by express invitation of the Queen I was there. In the autumn of the previous year the Duchess had arranged for me to meet the Queen at Balmoral, and I went there for a very brief interview. She was an extraordinary figure, short and squat, wearing a plain black skirt, a loose jacket, and a mushroom hat, tied with a big ribbon bow under her chin. She asked me a few questions about my children, and then invited me to come to the next Drawing-Room. Most people who knew her had something to say about her dignity, and she had a most commanding eye. But in Court dress, and wearing her crown, she looked a little grotesque—not like Queen Alexandra or Queen Mary, both of whom looked truly regal in Court dress.

Only the very strong could enjoy the rigours of a March Court at Buckingham Palace in those days. First, the long wait in the Mall; in these days there was no thermos providing comforting hot drinks, and no refreshments of any kind, not even a cup of tea, in the Palace. Certainly there was a fire in the large dressing-room, but the toilet arrangements were ghastly—in fact, they were non-existent. We were always thankful when it was a small attendance, so that we could get quickly away. But four hours was the usual length of the ordeal.

When King Edward and Queen Alexandra inaugurated the evening Courts, with their warmth and brilliance, the kind consideration for the comfort of the guests, everybody acclaimed the change. But nobody grumbled, except privately, in Victoria's time. It was the age which covered up things, and endured without visible revolt.

I have wondered often whether the Queen would have been so gracious to me if she had known of my friendship, if I may use that word, with Mr. Gladstone. I did not see any of the Gladstones on the two occasions I attended a Victorian Court, but, of course, attendance of ministers of the Crown was not compulsory, except possibly once during the season. Doubtless, at their age, they would prefer a summer Court.

During these years I carried on considerable correspondence with the Duchess, while she was at Dunkeld. By some deplorable accident, or carelessness, a great bundle of her letters got burned among other things when we were breaking up the house after Dr. Burnett Smith's death. It was a real catastrophe, for extracts from them would have added grace and charm to these pages. They were real letters, full of wise counsel and witty comments on passing events. Her beautiful, clear calligraphy, her expressive phrases, and above all, the meticulous care with which she wrote, as if it were a pleasure and not a task, set me an excellent example. Those were the days when letter-writing was an art, to which people did not hesitate to devote both time and pains. Of course there was more leisure.

To one so restless and adventurous as myself it was a revelation and ought to have been an example to witness how these two ladies lived out their lives in such orderly sequence. Once, when we were there, I was astounded to hear Miss Murray Macgregor say that they were two weeks back with their *Scotsmans* and would have to tackle them to come up to date. Nobody would read a two-weeks-old newspaper nowadays. They were nothing if not thorough in every department of their lives.

It is not easy in a book of this kind to observe the perfect sequence as practised by these ladies of the old school.

Amulree naturally suggested association with Dunkeld, and so to London in advance. We did not reach London for a year or two after our introduction to Dunkeld.

That was the last year of my husband's student life, and when it was over he was very tired, and though we could not well afford it, indeed had no business to be spending the money on travel at all, we went to Ober-Ammergau to see the Passion Play. It was money well spent, for the holiday among the mountains restored us completely both in health and spirits.

I did not like the Passion Play. I came out before the end. The Old Testament scenes interested me, as any historical pageant might, but I could not bear the intimate presentation of our Lord's life and sufferings by any human beings, however consecrated and reverent their mien. My husband sat it out to the end, and it greatly impressed him. We had lodgings in the house of John the Baptist, and the life of the villagers interested me far more than the play.

The seething crowds, the commonplace people bartering jokes on Biblical themes, though they would be bathed in tears at the play, struck on my mind and heart a bizarre, repellent note. How many of these weeping onlookers made any real attempt to follow in the footsteps of the Man of Nazareth ? Theirs were facile tears, such as flow easily and leave little impression behind. Many do not agree with this conclusion, of course, but that was how it affected me.

We left Musselburgh and Scotland the next spring, when my husband, having taken his degree, had now to address himself to the practice of his profession.

Though London was our goal, he felt the need of some practical experience first, so he took a post as assistant to a very busy doctor in the Black Country, at a place called Lye, near Stourbridge, in Worcestershire. It was a purely industrial neighbourhood, among chain-makers and nail-makers, and the six months there gave him more experience of general practice than he could have got anywhere else.

He made good there, so good that the doctor implored him to stay on, offering him partnership and succession on very favourable terms. But for me, he would, I think, have accepted it, but it was an appalling place to live in. I could not resign myself to spending my life there. Perhaps it was a mistake, for he had one or two lean years in London before he got established. And yet I don't know.

The older I grow and the more I ponder on the mystery of life, the more firmly I am convinced of the

> " Divinity that shapes our ends,
>   Rough hew them how we will."

I wrote there my novel *A Bitter Debt : A Story of the Black Country.*

CHAPTER SIX

LONDON LIFE

WE established our first London home at 52 Camden Square, N.W. These old squares, which abound in North London, have a charm of their own, and were delightful to live in before they began to suffer that strange dry rot which seems to overtake all city areas sooner or later.

The houses were roomy and dignified, though all of them had basements, that bugbear of the modern housewife. So long as nobody has to sleep down there, a basement has some advantages. It ensures a dry house, and quiet in the upstairs regions. Ours was only a semi-basement, opening out to the garden at the back. It had been a doctor's house for a long time and had wonderful surgeries and waiting-rooms, with an entrance in a side street.

The price asked for the lease and the practice a very slender one, for the incumbent (an Aberdeen man) had sadly neglected it, was two thousand pounds. We had saved a little, and an old friend of the family, Mr. John Bell of Balbuthie, lent us a thousand pounds without interest, and no security except the house and his faith in us. I have often

5

marvelled at the light-hearted way in which we assumed these heavy responsibilities. Nothing daunts youth at the prow. But we were both earning now. I had a steady income from my serial work in the *People's Friend*, and the future seemed fairly well assured.

The practice wanted working up, and after the appalling strenuousness of life at the branch practice in the Black Country, my husband felt himself entirely at a loose end. He was not very happy those days, chafing at his semi-idleness and inclined to regret having missed such a splendid chance as had been offered him. I was not very happy either, as can be imagined, having been the deciding factor in his rejection of the offer. However, as time went on things improved. He was a tireless worker, and a born healer, who inspired confidence the moment he entered a sick-room. His patients were not only cases but human beings, and he gave the same devoted attention to them all, whether they were rich or poor.

I delighted in getting the house in order. I have often said that I am prouder of being a good house-wife than of my literary reputation. The greatest compliment I ever had paid was by a man who told me I could make a home out of a cave and a handful of twigs. Our friends and relations who came to see us were charmed with our new home and its surroundings. The spacious square garden, with its spreading trees, gave us, in summer, the illusion of rural surroundings.

There are few aspects of London life more mysterious and perplexing than the decay of residential areas. Sometimes they come again, as in the case of Bloomsbury, which for a time became quite fashionable.

We were very happy in Camden Square, for there our two children were born. A great sorrow befel us in our first London year in the death of my father, who had removed from the farm to an Edinburgh house, where he continued his business as a potato merchant.

We were in Switzerland when he died, having accepted an invitation to join the Henry Lunn tourist party, at which I had to give a paper in return for our entertainment. We found ourselves in very good company. Conan Doyle was one of the party, also Benjamin Waugh, the founder of the Society for the Prevention of Cruelty to Children, and the Price Hughes. I think that must have been Conan Doyle's first lecturing experience, for he was obviously very nervous.

We hurried back to London, but were too late to see my father in life. I did not travel north for the funeral, as Effie was then on the way, and the hurried journey had tired me out. I mourned my father sincerely, and deeply regretted that he had never been able to make the journey to see our London house, in which he took such a keen and affectionate interest. One of his old letters contained much good advice about saving and "going slow," with particular reference to the horse

" Jeems " had taken over with the practice. We had to put down the carriage immediately, however. It was a luxury the practice could not yet afford to maintain.

The last time I bade him good-bye at Waverley Station he was a very gentle, rather pathetic old man, who dwelt much in the past. Tears stood in his eyes as the train steamed out. I was deeply touched to learn that, in his last illness, my mother's name was often on his lips. The dominator apparently was not able to dominate the inner citadel of his heart. He died very poor. In his time he had made and lost a lot of money, but did not know how to keep it together. I am a little like that myself, though in later years " needs must " has engendered in me some principles of economy.

In January 1893 our first child was born. Her arrival created considerable interest in my reading public. One of the joys of a rather tedious convalescence was receiving the gifts which poured in from all quarters, sent by people I had never seen nor ever expected to see. One anonymous gift, delivered by hand at the door, was a string of pearls. I thought they were only paste beads, looking very attractive in a velvet-lined case, but an expert assured me later that they were real and perfectly matched pearls. We never traced the donor.

Two years after his sister's birth our little son appeared, and it seemed then as if life had little more to offer.

There is no happier time in a woman's life than

EFFIE AND EDDIE (NANNIE)

when she has her little bairns about her knees. One perplexed and harassed mother of a grown-up family said to me one day :

" The only time it is worth while being a mother is when you can spank them when they are naughty and put them in their beds, where you know they are safe."

We had a faithful old Cockney nurse whose way with young children I have never seen equalled. But her accent was deplorable, and she had to be dispensed with soon after they began to talk. She went from us to Lady Robertson Nicoll, who, of course, found the same quite unsurmountable difficulty.

Nanna was succeeded by Ellen Hazel, a mother's help who for several years, indeed until the children were ready for school, was an enormous help. She was quite a treasure in the house ; so kindly, efficient, and faithful that we still remember her with gratitude and affection.

The five years we spent in Camden Square were crowded with new experiences. In the full tide of life and health, I was avid for them. I was naturally eager to come in contact with other writers, and looked forward eagerly to much stimulating and helpful interchange of thought and experience. Rather a vain delusion, I found. Writing people as a rule, are not great or even interesting talkers, and the very last thing they want to discuss is their ideals, if they have any. I found literary society rather dull, though there were, of course,

bright exceptions, which linger with fragrance in
one's memory.

Mankind in the mass, whether cabbages or kings,
is much alike.

Many who have given immortal works to the
world have studiously shunned the company of
their fellow-men. They choose the country, when
possible, for residence, and refuse to herd in crowds.
Meredith, Hardy, Mark Rutherford are some of
the contemporary names occurring in this relation.

It is the lesser lights who have no objection to
blazing in concert.

There were numerous literary clubs in those days
—the Savage, the Yorick, and the Vagabonds—
whose popularity killed it. The Fabian Society
came into being about that time, but I think its
portals were closed to women, at first, at least.

There used to be delightful tea parties at the
offices of *The Idler*, a magazine which had a considerable vogue. I was often a guest there, and
among those who forgathered were Anthony Hope,
Zangwill, Conan Doyle, and his brother-in-law,
Hornung, the creator of Raffles, Barry Pain,
W. W. Jacobs, the Leightons, Richard Whiteing,
the Corkrans, Alice and Henriette, and many
others.

To me the light badinage, the rapier-like thrusts,
the frank, outspoken criticism were very stimulating.
I was far too shy to take part. There was, I think,
very little serious talk. Problems did not loom
so largely as in this generation. I think we were

all agreed that the business of life was to live. And
we certainly lived with all our might.

Even then the women writers were as the sands
of the sea for multitude. Among the stars then
high in the literary world were Mrs. Humphrey Ward,
Lucas Malet, Mrs. W. K. Clifford, Sarah Grand,
Violet Hunt, Mrs. Stannard (" John Strange
Winter "), Mrs. Mannington Caffyn, who wrote *The
Yellow Aster*, Beatrice Harraden. Among poets we
had Mrs. Meynell and Mrs. Woods.

The great event of our particular literary year
was the Women Writers' Dinner, which took place
usually at the Trocadero Restaurant. When the
idea first originated in the fertile and progressive
brain of Honor Morten, much fun was made of it
in the press. It was " news " of the first order,
and we certainly got, without effort, all the publicity
we wanted — sometimes more. The Feminist
Movement, called in those ancient days the " Revolt
of Women," was just beginning to express itself.
Mona Caird had thrown a flaming bomb into the
camp of the thoroughly smug and respectable
ranks with an article in the *Daily Telegraph* called
" Is Marriage a Failure ? "

Violent correspondence raged round that for
months, even years, and she was banned and
shunned like the plague in certain circles. Then
Sarah Grand published *The Heavenly Twins*, dealing
with sex questions and the operation of venereal
disease in family life, treated with a frankness which
appalled the Victorians. I can remember the

occasion on which she was to act as chairman at the Dinner, the committee met and gravely decided that she should be asked to carefully avoid touching on such a debatable subject, and leave Man out of her speech. She was furious, and her speech, in consequence, was both brief—and not brotherly.

I sometimes wonder what she thinks of it all now in her dignified retirement at Bath.

In due course I took my turn as chairman, no mean ordeal to face a hundred critical women and say the right thing. It was always an interesting occasion, to which we all looked forward with eager anticipation. The old idea that women dressed for men was completely exploded. We all wore our very best frocks, and it was a very attractive crowd. An attempt to revive this famous dinner was made some years after the war, but it was a dismal failure I journeyed from Scotland for the event, but felt as if I were in the company of ghosts. A more depressing evening could not be imagined, though desperate attempts to illumine it were made by some of the new stars in the literary firmament. Something lacked, I don't know what. It will never happen again. There is always a certain risk attached to such revivals. Generally speaking, they prove a disappointing mistake.

Mrs. Humphrey Ward represented the dignity of letters. She moved in august circles and did not consort much with the lesser crowd. She took herself very seriously, and had not much sympathy with the Bohemian element, which adds so much

to the gaiety of nations.   I find in one of her letters
some trace of uneasiness regarding her chairmanship
at the Dinner.

" GROSVENOR PLACE,
" *June* 26, 1900.

" I was very glad to be at the Dinner last night,
but am afraid my speech was rather heavy for the
occasion.   But it seemed best to write and speak
as is most natural to me.   I wish you would come
and talk over the dinner and other things.   If you
could tell me a good deal more about the people
who were there last night I should be glad.

" I am afraid that owing partly to health, partly
to work, I do not know as much of those who are
now struggling with literary work as I ought to
know.   We are very much in the country, and the
Settlement in Tavistock Place, of which I was one
of the founders, absorbs a great deal of my time
outside literary occupation.

" Yet I am sure that we, who are engaged in this
arduous work, can do much to cheer and sympathise
with one another."

No one could associate Mrs. Humphrey Ward
with any kind of struggle.   She appeared to have
everything in her favour, yet her sympathy with
the less fortunate was warm and true, or she would
not have given so much of herself to the Tavistock
Place Settlement.

Of that bright galaxy, which illumined the
Bohemian firmament in these days, very few are

left, and these are chiefly living in retirement, not
making any contribution to the world of letters.

They have been crowded out by the vast regiment
of women who are engaged in producing the modern
novel, which no doubt reflects the passing show, the
mood and manners of the time, as accurately as the
old writers presented theirs.

How great and wide is the difference, and one
may well ask—Whither Britain ? Though I have
marched with the times, I am still a Victorian in this,
that I deplore the complete overthrow of dignity and
reticence, which has left us neither shrine nor holy
place. For greed of gain every experience of
humanity and life is exploited in the market-place.
Our deepest feelings, all our inhibitions have become
mere merchandise. Perhaps it is all to the good,
and we shall emerge in consequence a finer and
stronger race. I wonder ?

The Boer War happened while we were living in
Camden Square. It was not like the Great War,
which the nation felt as one man. There were extraordinary and violent differences of opinion as to the
rights and wrongs of it. Those who thought Britain
had no right to attack were called Pro-Boers and
more loathed by the Jingoes than the pacifists were
in the Great War. An old friend of mine, Mr.
Thomas Shaw, now Lord Craigmyle, suffered genuine
persecution for his strong pro-Boer views. His
house in Edinburgh was broken into and his desk
ransacked for evidence that he had been a traitor to
his country. I wrote a series of short stories of

the war, under another name, for the *British Weekly*, and they created a good deal of interest.

Years after, Rosslyn Mitchell told me that they were regularly read and debated by the young men in the Glasgow Literary Society to which he belonged. They were supposed to have been written either by a member of the military staff, or a journalist on the spot. When he asked me how I, a mere woman, sitting snugly at my desk in London, could have achieved them, I could only reply that I was a faithful student of the war correspondents' columns, studied the map, and imagination did the rest. It all distressed me frightfully, and two incidents stand out. One black day when news of the *débâcle* of the Highlanders at Magersfontein came, I was in an Underground train. Reading the dispatch in an early edition of the evening paper, I turned and made some desperate remark to the well-dressed woman beside me. She stared at me vacantly, and said :

" What war ?   I didn't know there was a war ! "

A little later I happened to be fulfilling a public engagement of some sort at Southampton, and was the guest of the Hon. Mrs. Eliot York at Hamble Cliff. She took me to Netley Hospital to see the few wounded men who had survived the terrible affair at Magersfontein.

Never shall I forget the impression made by the sight of their prostrate figures, with bandaged heads, part of the aftermath of war. Little did I dream how familiar such sights were to become in the dark days to come.

Among my treasures I find a little snapshot taken by my husband's old friend, Sir Watson Cheyne, the surgeon, who was on Lord Roberts staff all through the campaign. It was taken on the field when poor old Kruger surrendered to the victorious general, a pitiful figure, not in the least heroic, though slightly patriarchal. There was neither glory nor glamour about that surrender or that victory.

But is there ever any in war? Surely all the false glitter which once surrounded it has been exploded for ever!

CHAPTER SEVEN

THE WOMAN AT HOME

I WORKED hard with my pen during those early years in London. It was necessary, for though my husband was soon earning a substantial income, our expenses were constantly increasing. We were both lavish spenders. We loved beautiful things, and Jim's taste in pictures and furniture led him into all sorts of extravagances. He spent all his leisure in antique shops, to the detriment of his pocket, though our home benefited.

I remember the first time the Robertson Nicolls came to see us, how surprised they were with our domicile. He smiled and said dryly : " It's the celerity with which you have amassed large pieces of furniture." I hastened to explain that we had taken over a good deal from the last incumbent, and that only the drawing-room was new.

After the children were born, we realised that for their sakes, as well as our own, it was necessary to establish some sort of permanent connection with Scotland. We had a small cottage at Kinghorn, a little, grey, old-world village on the Forth. It had a glorious outlook and a perfect beach. One of the oldest burghs in Scotland, it has much historical interest. The old harbour at Pettycur was once the place where travellers from Fife embarked for Leith and Edinburgh—the only alternative being the circuitous road journey round by Stirling.

There was a little inn at Pettycur, a " howff " known to a few discerning ones—among them William Sharp ("Fiona Macleod "), who was often there with a kindred soul or two. He always dropped in to see us, a big Viking of a man, with a shock of fair hair and very blue eyes. We often saw him and his delightful wife after we were all settled in London. Never was literary secret better kept than the identity of Fiona Macleod. It was known to three or four people over a long period of years, but was not divulged till after his death. I have all his books on my shelves now. As the interpreter of the sorrow and the mysticism of the Isles Fiona Macleod has no equal.

We acquired a narrow building site on the cliff overhanging the sea, and proceeded to erect the house. Fools build houses, they say, and wise men live in them. I must be numbered among the fools in this respect, for I have helped to build five houses in my time. It is a fascinating game, but never a paying one. It is possible to drop more money on real estate than in any other form of speculation, because it is impossible to bank on a neighbourhood not deteriorating or undergoing drastic change.

THE ANCHORAGE, KINGHORN

Kinghorn has changed out of all recognition. It became one of the defences of the Forth in the war, and was part of the danger zones. Now it is wholly given up to campers and trippers, and all that is left to me of bitter-sweet memory is the grave on the windy hill where my loved ones sleep.

But for many years The Anchorage was a joy to us. Our children spent long, golden summers there and loved it with a great love. We were fortunate in having my sister Janet, the only unmarried one of the Mountskip band, make her permanent home there, so that it was open and ready for us at any time. My two younger sisters, Mary and Margaret, met their future husbands in Kinghorn, which would seem to bear out the conception of the Destiny which shapes our ends.

These were busy, fruitful years, in which my chief adviser and encourager in literary matters was Sir William Robertson Nicoll. I had had some correspondence with him before we left Scotland, and several short stories from my pen had appeared in the *British Weekly*, then in the full tide of its triumphant success.

He was an extraordinary man. Meredith is reported to have described himself as the possessor of at least six personalities. I am sure Robertson Nicoll had as many. I knew him intimately over a period of years, while we were neighbours in Hampstead and my husband the medical attendant of the family, but I could not attempt a portrait of him. He was a staunch and wonderful friend, but he had hosts of enemies, being ruthless in criticism and less than any man I have ever met " able to suffer fools gladly."

He had a marvellous flair for discovering literary talent. It was his habit to carefully scan the pages of provincial newspapers, and when arrested by any contribution—verse, article, or story—to make a note of it and unearth the writer. He could trace the origin of anything, no matter how obscure. I was often astounded by it.

No doubt Sir James Barrie would have arrived without him, but his arrival must have been hastened by Nicoll's warm and quick appreciation. He discovered Crockett too, and Ian Maclaren. Apparently he had watched my progress and noted my contributions to the *Christian Leader*. He had a warm admiration for Howie Wylie, recognising in him a kindred spirit, with the same flair for literature and the same passion for books.

One day he came to me with rather a startling proposition. He thought there was room for a new woman's magazine, and he wanted me to be associated with it—not as Editor, where I should have been a dismal failure (owing to the tendency to allow my heart to govern my head), but as chief contributor, and to have my name printed on the cover.

For years the magazine was popularly known as *Annie Swan's Magazine.*

Of course I was only too happy to agree, and thus began one of the most interesting chapters in my writing life.

The outstanding feature of the magazine was the correspondence columns, which I conducted under the heading " Over the Teacups." It was an instant and overwhelming success. The letters used to be sent from the office to my house, if not literally in sacks, at least in gigantic bundles. Queer stuff they were ! The effect on me at first was disastrous. I could not sleep at night, convinced by these poignant effusions that the whole of creation was groaning and travailing in anguish. It was quite a long time before I got inured to my task, which taught me more about the seamy side of life than I had imagined existed before. It was an interesting study in psychology and could have provided material for hundreds of novels. Either I knew in a flash what to say, or could say nothing at all. I often felt that a Father Confessor was needed in many lives, some one remote and unattached, who could be trusted to offer unbiased judgment.

I must here pay tribute to the enormous help Dr. Burnett Smith was able to give me in dealing with this voluminous correspondence. Much of the trouble could be traced to physical causes, then the man's point of view was invaluable, preventing sentiment from overruling sound judgment.

Love affairs and matrimonial squabbles and problems provided then, as now, the main theme of the letters. My sheet anchor was the constant reminder that every story has two sides. Some of them were extraordinary stories, quite often the essence of comedy.

6

For instance, a couple resident in Cumberland wrote quite seriously, explaining that they were getting on very badly and could I come and pay them a short visit to tell them what was the matter. I did not lack courage, but I had not sufficient for that. The one who seeks to arbitrate between man and wife usually gets the bulk of the blows. Besides, as I pointed out, a personal visit would be futile as, out of politeness, they would be obliged to behave in front of me. Apparently they had no idea or intention of separating. People didn't then, except for the major cause. Married people put up with things, bearing in mind the significance of the vow, " For better for worse."

There was, of course, a lot of sex stuff in these letters. They were an education to me in the sordid side of life. Whether the advice I so conscientiously handed out did any good I doubt very much, as the only advice people want is that which coincides with their own opinions and desires. But these correspondence columns certainly interested the public. Many men have told me that they never missed reading them.

Alice Head, now the distinguished director of the National Magazine Company, and certainly the ablest editress in London, was for several years on the staff of the *Woman at Home*. We all loved her, and our friendship has lasted to this day.

The *Woman at Home*, which did not survive the Great War, provided a fruitful and steady source of income for a good many years. They were the most productive years of my life, and had we been content to plod on in Camden Square would have amassed a considerable competency, which would have ensured ease and luxury in our old age. But we were not built that way, nor did we ever pause to consider that our respective professions were entirely personal, and that, should capacity fail, there would be no assets left behind it.

Possibly because we had been poor so long, having had to count every penny before spending it, when money came, it simply slipped through our fingers. How we enjoyed spending! And in the process acquired books and pictures and other beautiful things to adorn our home.

I regret nothing. It was all experience which, generally speaking, has to be bought in the dearest market.

Then there were many needing help, and we were glad to help. That kind of service is one of the sweetest things life has to offer. We saw eye to eye about that, and when we used to be making up the quarterly bills to be sent out to the patients, how often the Doctor would say :

" Oh, I can't send that. They couldn't pay it without an awful effort," and would then cut down the claim by about half. Afterwards, when an enormous practice necessitated a partner, he could not do that. But other ways of helping were easily discovered.

We were only contented in Camden Square for about five years. The steady decline of the neighbourhood was apparent. Whenever a large house became vacant, it was broken up into flats or apartments, which brought an entirely different class of people about us. We were as ambitious for our children as for ourselves, and our thoughts began to turn towards the heights of Hampstead, where we had many friends.

The Doctor sold his house and practice without difficulty, for it was now a flourishing concern, and with the proceeds we acquired a house at Hampstead and simply squatted to wait for new business to come.

It was a tedious process, and he often regretted the step he had taken, though he never reproached me with having urged the change. However, in the end he achieved success, though some of the dark days were difficult to live through. It was a growing neighbourhood, and a few successful cases helped to establish him. He was a born surgeon, and if we had had enough money, he would have specialised in surgery. However, his chance came later, in an unexpected way.

CHAPTER EIGHT

HAMPSTEAD DAYS

WHEN we went to live at Hampstead, the Finchley Road beyond West End Lane was a green country way, bordered by ragged hedges, with white may bloom and wild roses in summer.

One of my children's treats was to be taken for a ride on the top of the green horse omnibus which plied between the Finchleys and Baker Street.

Though signs of the monstrous exploitation of that attractive district were not lacking, there were no houses except certain old mansions between Child's Hill and Finchley. Now Golders Green, a city in itself, is linked up with both Finchley and Hendon. Greater London has indeed pushed itself out, until those who love the country have to go farther and farther afield to find it. Old Hampstead proper has suffered less, being saved by the Heath and the strict laws forbidding any encroachment on it.

Hampstead has always been beloved of artists and writing folk. The Nicolls lived at Baytree Lodge, a delectable old house in Frognal Lane, within a stone's-throw of the parish church and

Church Row, with its beautiful old, tree-shaded houses.

Walter Besant lived at Frognal End, the Du Mauriers, the Quiller-Couches, Beatrice Harraden, and others close by. Hampstead indeed was then rich in literary flavour, established long before our time. We were incomers and had to be content with a new house, for business purposes, nearer the main thoroughfare.

Sir William's first wife, whom he married in Kelso, was a woman of great charm and distinction, beloved by all who knew her. Her untimely death left him with two young children at the mercy of hired help. A more utterly helpless being in household affairs could not be imagined, and after a run of acute domestic difficulty and discomfort, he married Miss Katherine Pollard of High Down, Hitchin, who, by her grace and sweet kindliness, quickly restored the atmosphere of home to Baytree Lodge.

It was a very happy marriage, and Lady Robertson Nicoll retired in her widowhood to the Old Manse at Lumsden, where her husband was born. There was one child of the second marriage, now the wife of Captain Grange Kirkcaldy, Lodge of Auchendoir, Rhynie. Our children and the Nicolls were inseparable, and the friendship continues, warm and comforting, to this day.

Sooner or later, everybody who was anybody came to Baytree Lodge. Scots authors were often in the foreground. We met Sir James Barrie frequently, also Ian Maclaren and that stormy petrel Crockett, who was always dashing up from Penicuik to London on some pretext or other. He did not long continue in the ministry of the Free Church of Scotland after he took to the writing life. He was a queer mixture, with something most lovable about him.

Among my old letters I find this characteristic one of his :

"BANK HOUSE, PENICUIK,
"*May*, 1894.

"MY DEAR ANNIE SWAN,—It is Saturday. I have two sermons to preach to-morrow, neither done. I have a story proof to send off. We are in the hubbub of flitting, camping among boxes. *But* I sit down to write a word of thanks for *Elizabeth Glen*. I don't often read stories in magazines except those in proof by a raider called Crockett. But I read your 'Barbara' with great enjoyment, standing first on one leg then on the other. Why, Dr. E. Glen well knows. I'm but a poor truth-teller who, like yourself, makes a scanty living by telling lies. I can only state facts. Why do geese sleep standing on one leg ? That is the reason I read your 'Barbara' standing thus.

"Seriously, I did enjoy the story, nor have I forgotten the pleasant afternoon with the teller and her lord.

"Mirree sends her love.   S. R. C."

Here is one more :

" MY DEAR ANNIE SWAN,—It seems a long time
since we heard from you.   My fault of course.   But
you promised to let me hear how you got on in the
chair at the Women Writers' Dinner, where I heard
you made the Yellow Asters wilt, and ' Ships that
pass in the Night ' to hasten on as fast as they
could.

" Though you don't tell us, you did nobly, we
heard, and Mirree cried ' Huzza, an' gie her
anither ! '

" We also heard you've been in Scotland without
coming to see us.   We've had the Barries and
Andrew Lang quite often.   But Doctor and Mrs.
Burnett Smith never !   What do you mean by it ?
Meeting you is always an oasis in London.   Your
home life looks so true and fresh and Scottish to me,
like coming home unexpectedly after a sea voyage
and finding you at the front gate.

" I am correcting proofs of my Covenanting tale
for *Good Words*.   The *Lilac* has done well, twenty-
six thousand in twenty days !   The world loves a
love story yet !   Come soon and make happy two
plain folk living quietly in the country.

" S. R. C."

We lost touch with our friend in later years, and
those in Hampstead to whom he had meant a good
deal mourned when he turned his back on his native
land for ever.

Among the letters I find several from Sir James Barrie, who did not write voluminously even to friends.   Here is a sample :

" I feel so melancholy at party functions and I haven't been to any for years.   If I went to any I'd come to yours, but some day I'm going to drop in for that game of billiards."

Another, in reply to one I had written after reading *Margaret Ogilvy* :

" Your letter has given me great pleasure.
" I shall be well satisfied if the book calls up such memories to others, and if it shewed them another force.   For if it has any value at all, it is because it is about not one, but many mothers.   Come in and see us any day at tea-time.   I speak now for two."

" I shall be so pleased if you will come and support me at the Literary Fund Dinner.   It is the first time ladies have been invited and I am anxious to make a brave beginning."

A week later :

" I am slowly recovering from being a chairman. There were some few there on whose sincerity I could take my oath.   You were one.   It is the salt of our calling, and of all others.
" J. M. BARRIE."

.   .   .   .   .

One night at one of the weird crushes Douglas Sladen used to give in his Kensington flat, I found myself jammed in the passage beside a melancholy-looking individual whom I had no difficulty in recognising as Hall Caine.

We stood there for about twenty minutes talking. At least, he talked and I listened. If you wish to commend yourself to any man, let him talk about himself; all you require to do is to listen with a moderate amount of intelligence.

I was prodigiously entertained, for he was an interesting personality, who took himself and his work very seriously.

To my surprise, a week or so later, I received a copy of *The Eternal City* and a letter from Greeba Castle, in which he thanked me warmly for the delightful conversation we had had at Sladen's party. There was no conversation, only an oration to an audience of one, but I greatly enjoyed the book and wrote to tell him so. His reply was as follows :

" GREEBA CASTLE, ISLE OF MAN.

" MY DEAR ANNIE SWAN,—I am addressing you by the name whereby the world knows you. Your letter came at a moment when I was feeling greatly depressed under the wilful, as well as, in some cases, unconscious misrepresentation to which I am being exposed on all sides.

" So warm, so tender, so sincerely felt a tribute to my book (*The Eternal City*) could not fail to bring comfort. I thank you for the impulse which sent it. If it were worth while, I might say something of the misjudging my book has gone through, not on the literary side only. That was to be expected, but on the side of the intellectual intention, its political, its religious, and above all, its purely human motive. I don't know if you are subjected to these trying experiences ? I understand that, notwithstanding your great success, you have not been assailed, although it seems difficult to believe that even the most amiable woman can altogether escape the shafts of jealousy.

" For my own part, I have ceased to feel personally hurt, but this does not save one from the loss of heart which comes of seeing the deepest thing on one's purpose misrepresented and belied. I have to be grateful for such letters as yours, from the best intellects and the truest-hearted natures.—Yours always,

" HALL CAINE."

He somewhat resembled Marie Corelli in temperament. They were both self-centred and supersensitive, imagining slights were none were intended.

I have always been thankful to be free from that form of handicap. I have suffered all sorts of snubs and slights in my time, some of which would have sent these two good friends of mine crazy. But they never lingered long in my memory, nor did I ever suffer them to darken my day. I accepted them as part of the discipline of life. So I have never had any enemies, at least I have not discovered them, whereas Marie Corelli found them on every bush, so to speak. When I found people either hostile or aloof, I just left them alone. And sometimes by some mysterious process they were converted into friends.

I suppose this sort of easy-going philosophy is not possible to the born fighter. Any talks I had with Marie Corelli both in London and at her lovely house at Stratford-on-Avon were punctuated by tales of persecution and bad treatment she had received, chiefly from persons engaged in her own craft.

In one letter I find this sentence : " In spite of slander and misrepresentation I forgive as quickly as I forget, and am only too pleased if I can make ' even an enemy ' happy for a moment."

She looked at me in astonishment when I said one day it was better not to have any enemies ; they served no useful purpose.

She was really " agin' " most things as well as people. One day my daughter and I had promised to lunch with her and had a lot of correspondence about such a simple affair. The Government summer-time worried her. " I never have conformed to it and never will," she wrote, " but we can arrange that you lunch quite comfortably if you will let me know what time you are bound to leave us. I daresay it will amuse you to know that I do not conform to the upsetting of the sundial and

Greenwich time. Except when one is obliged to catch trains it is not necessary to allow Government to force you to get up with a lie, and go to bed with one—*i.e.* to call 6 a.m. 7, and 9 p.m. 10 p.m."

But in spite of that queer strain in her I liked her, and always found her both kind and interesting to talk to.

She was very proud that King Edward was a reader and admirer of her books, and one of her treasures was a very large signed picture of him which hung in the hall at Mason Croft.

She missed a great deal by dwelling on her imaginary wrongs ; one by one even friends became estranged ; and at the end I am afraid she was one of the loneliest souls on earth.

The public is a relentless judge and critic. More and more I am convinced that human beings only get out of life what they put into it.

CHAPTER NINE

MORE HAMPSTEAD DAYS

SO much has been written about Sir William Robertson Nicoll that any words of mine seem superfluous. But as it is the story of my own life I am writing, I must of necessity deal with those who influenced me. His encouragement, criticism, and help were certainly of enormous value to me in my work, for unfortunately I was born with a considerable share of the " inferiority complex " the moderns talk so much about, and have always been easily discouraged, and too ready to conclude that I have failed, or am going to fail, in anything I attempt. It is almost as disastrous to achievement as overweening conceit. Nicoll believed in me, and for those who believe in us are we not ready to do our very best ? As an Editor I have never met any one like him.

He had one outstanding quality, very rare in Editors—he never meddled with your work. Having given you the commission, which he believed you capable of undertaking, he left you to execute it according to the light that was in you.

I remarked on this to him one day, and his answer was :

" You don't need anybody to teach you your job."

This latitude, so freely allowed, did not mean any slackness on his part. He had no quarter for slackness or carelessness. He demanded and expected the best. A tireless and most methodical worker himself, with a memory of terrifying range and accuracy, any plea of forgetfulness roused him to fury.

" Forgot ! Don't tell me you forgot ! It is only an aggravation of the offence."

The *British Weekly* was his life-work and his idol. He started other things, but quickly tired of them, but the *British Weekly* he loved and laboured for to the last. It was his genius which conceived and established it, and for many its savour departed when that marvellous pen was stilled for ever.

It is impossible to speak of the *British Weekly* without reference to Miss Jane T. Stoddart, his able and devoted colleague. She was far and away the most accomplished woman journalist I have ever met—widely read, mistress of several languages, author of many thoughtful and wise books. She is still at her post. I valued her friendship. She was so loyal and kind and helpful always.

One day, not long after we went to Hampstead, Sir William said to me :

" You have never got justice done to your work. They've set you in a groove. Let us create a new writer in the *British Weekly*.

So David Lyall was born.

The secret was well kept for a great many years, and until now I have never openly acknowledged my part in the harmless plot. There was much speculation regarding the new author. Sir William himself was even accused of being the culprit. It was " David " who wrote the Boer War stories, hence the confusion in the minds of the Glasgow young men.

One day one of my sisters went into an Edinburgh bookseller's to purchase a copy of *The Land o' the Leal*, the first collection of short stories, which had attracted some attention in the *British Weekly*. Handling the book, she said casually : " Some say Annie Swan wrote this."

Great surprise and contempt from the salesman, who replied indignantly : " Annie Swan ! She couldn't touch it ! "

Which just shows—well, what does it show ? I leave it at that.

It was certainly true that quite early in life I was set in a groove, wherein I was expected to stop, writing serious and innocuous fiction for the de- lectation of babes. It is not so easy to preserve the required flavour, after one is engulfed by the full tide of life and become a part of its moving panorama. However, I have done my best, and with one exception, which will be dealt with in a later chapter, have been able to please my large and loyal public.

Our life in Hampstead was like a moving picture.

We were entertained a lot, and entertained ourselves on a considerable scale. They were the days of the monstrous, interminable dinners, of ten or twelve courses. Very few accomplished the feat of eating steadily through the menu. Nevertheless, hostesses vied with one another in securing something new and startling both in food and decorations. One of the few real services the war rendered was to simplify our dinner-tables, and put food in its proper place.

I plunged into the dinner game with real zest, fortifying myself with a course of French cookery so that I might bring expert knowledge to bear on the kitchen. I was a good mixer too, and having a wide circle of friends and acquaintances did not commit the crime of getting the wrong people together.

Looking back, now that I have returned permanently to the simpler life, it all seems a queer stupid sort of effort to have made. And yet it had its part to play. A writer must have some working knowledge of what he or she attempts to portray. It is so easy to detect the amateur or the person who has only second-hand information about people or things. No mere smattering satisfied me. I had to get the assurance only knowledge can give.

More and more I regret not having kept a diary through these vivid days, like my old friend Lord Riddell, who has given us so much inside information about the conduct of the war. I should certainly have had many rich titbits for there

pages. But I was so busy living just then, I had
no time to take notes. I can remember a few
occasions, but even a cultivated memory cannot
retain all it would.

One night at our dinner-table, there was an odd
interlude.

Gertrude Atherton, the American novelist, was
sitting by Dr. Parker of City Temple fame, and near
enough to me to permit me to hear part of their
conversation. They were discussing her new book,
American Wives and English Husbands, which Dr.
Nicoll had persuaded her to write. In such words
as these she described her difficulties with it, though
I cannot alas ! reproduce her vivid personality,
her beautiful face, and sparkling eyes.

" It's like this, see.   Dr. Nicoll told me I'd simply
got to write this book, and that nobody else could
do it—but somehow it wouldn't get going. So I
left London and went to a quiet little place on the
Normandy coast. Still nothing doing, and I was
about to give up the ghost, when one day I wandered
into the little church, where quite a few good women
were kneeling at their devotions. Why not join
them ? So down on my knees I gets to have a
private pow-wow with the Almighty. ' Oh, Lord,'
says I, ' this isn't fair. You gave me the gift which
I'm supposed to use, then you block it. If You
mean me to write this book, show me how.' Then
I went home and wrote it."

The dry smile on Dr. Parker's lips and the twinkle
in his eye indicated his keen enjoyment of this queer

challenge to the Almighty. She was a grandmother then, she told us, and though it was hard to credit it, she is still going strong in California, the home of her birth. This very month I read a powerful short story of hers in *Good Housekeeping*. I have heard that she is a triumphant example of some modern system of rejuvenation.

We were very intimate with the Parkers, and for years, both before and after Mrs. Parker's lamented and untimely death, I went to tea there every Saturday afternoon. It is seldom such well-known and brilliant people have so few friends. Dr. Parker did not encourage them. He lived the life of a recluse. It was the secret of his great ministry. He told me that one minister, trying to discover the secret of his success, received this answer :

" You talk all the week. I only talk on Sundays."

He was a great man, with a touch of genius, but in some respects very childlike, as the great so often are. We used to have terrific arguments, and fell out occasionally. He delighted in trying to rouse me to anger ; a not-too-easy task.

Once I stayed away three weeks, until I received a post card with this S.O.S. message in large print :

" Return, O wanderer, to thy home.
Thy Father calls for thee."

He had a great fund of humour. John Oliver Hobbes was one of the City Temple babies, and when she was received into the Roman Catholic Communion, she signed her letters to her old minister with the new name they had given her : " Pearl Mary Theresa Craigie."

Not to be outdone, Parker sent these words on a post card : " Affectionately, Matthew, Mark, Luke, John, Joseph Parker."

I often wondered what appeal the Catholic faith made to John Oliver Hobbes. She had a strong, vivid, brilliant personality, and both her books and her plays were considered very advanced in Victorian days. Her new faith required from her complete surrender to higher authority, and she was not by nature fitted to surrender anything gladly or easily. Her life was tragic in some aspects, culminating in the final blow which removed her in the zenith of her fame from the scenes and the profession she so much adorned.

The full story has never been told, though her mother lifted a portion of the veil when I saw her in the midst of her grief.

Only once did I hear John Oliver Hobbes make any comment on her change of faith. She described it thus :

" It is the overwhelming and comforting sense of peace which enfolds one when the surrender is made."

She used to disappear into retreat in the very height of the London season, throwing everything, even the most delectable engagements, to the wind when the summons came.

Surely now she has found the eternal peace she so ardently sought.

One night we had a big reception at our house to which Parker had refused to come. His lovely wife came, however, and about eleven o'clock one of the maids came to me, whispering that there was a funny old man on the doorstep, who refused to go away. I went out, to find my old friend, got him in, and soon he was the life and soul of the party. It did not break up very early. The majority left about midnight, but there was a remnant refusing to depart. I made tea for them at two o'clock in the morning.

I remember Zangwill, an odd little figure, hunched up in a corner of the sofa, saying languidly : " What a bore it must be to be God sitting up there, viewing the antics on this ant-heap."

Then they all fell to discussing what they would do, supposing they were miraculously invested with supreme power over the universe.

One Sunday afternoon in the Hampstead house I had a queer experience.

A friend called to see me, one quite well-known in the literary world. When I went down, she said she was glad to find me alone, and she seemed much upset. She began immediately :

" I've come to you because I've always said that if I needed a Father Confessor you'd be the one. I want to tell you that I have no more use for Charlie, and that I'm going to Paris on Tuesday night to meet G. We're everything to one another."

I collected my scattered wits, for the woman

outlining this programme I had imagined to be a
happy wife, with a perfectly good husband, and
some charming children. I knew that if I showed
the slightest sign of shock, disapproval, or alarm, I
should hear no more, so I said cheerfully :

" How thrilling ! Let's sit down and talk it
over."

We sat down, and she recited the sum of Charlie's
enormities, which seemed to consist chiefly in
having taken her for granted, after the manner of
husbands, and having failed to surround her with
a halo of attention and admiration. I listened,
speechless, until she had unburdened what was
certainly an overcharged heart. Then it was my
turn. I proceeded, not to comment at all on what
she had told me, but to draw a calm, reasoned, and
relentless picture of what was likely to happen in
the event of her carrying out her plan. I knew
G., and the kind of treatment he was likely to mete
out to any woman who had burned her boats for his
sake.

I pointed out that, having left a good home, a
sound husband, and a lovely family, she might
expect, say, six months of imagined happiness,
then the slow decline, ending in total extinction, of
G.'s selfish passion. Then she would be stranded,
probably with a new child on the way, and must
either live out an obscure life in some cheap con-
tinental resort, or come back to London, to face
what ? Those were Victorian days, remember,
when the divorcee was looked upon askance. Most

doors would be shut against her. She would find herself socially among the down-and-outs.

I didn't praise or defend Charlie, though I could have done. I simply appealed to her common sense, without offering any advice.

She stayed two mortal hours, and then she rose, thanked me for giving my time up to her, and went away. I felt pretty desperate, and even asked my husband whether I should try to warn Charlie. He said : " No. You've done all that is necessary. You can't betray a confidence like that."

I went down to the boat train on the Tuesday night, but saw no trace of the fugitive. The week passed, and Saturday came without a line or a sign. She " received " on Saturday afternoons, at her pretty house in Bayswater, so I repaired there, wondering what I should find.

To my amazement all was as usual, even to G. sitting in his accustomed corner, the husband, all unsuspecting, present too—the triangle complete ! The subject was never mentioned between us from that day to this, but the home was saved.

That's the stuff of life ! I had so much of it in London that there was no need to seek for imaginary plots. Nothing the imagination can conceive can equal in poignancy the happenings going on around us every day.

For a year I was President of the Women Journalists' Society, succeeding the brilliant Mrs. T. P. O'Connor. It was a most interesting, enlightening experience, bringing me into close personal touch with the working journalists, some of whom had hard lives.

Presiding at the Council meetings, month by month, I discovered in them none of the petty jealousies or meannesses with which our sex is so often falsely credited, but instead a passion for justice and fair dealing I have never seen excelled.

There was always a Presidential Dinner, and when my turn came I was anxious to get as many celebrities as possible to attend. I was specially anxious to get Marie Corelli, to see whether it would not be possible to pour some balm of Gilead on her difficult relations with the press. Her reply was characteristic :

" Those working journalists about whom you write so sweetly have so often painted the town red for me that no good purpose could possibly be served by trying to bring us together."

The speech of the evening was delivered by Lord Shaw of Dunfermline, now Lord Craigmyle, easily one of the best after-dinner speakers of his day.

We were great theatre-goers, first-nighters, when we had the chance. There were giants in those days—Irving and Ellen Terry in their prime, the Bancrofts, the Trees, the Kendals, John Hare, and Marie Tempest at the beginning of her brilliant career. Can one ever forget Ellen Terry's golden, heart-breaking voice as Ophelia or the delicious diablerie of her Madame Sans-Gêne ?

I had the privilege of being received by Sarah Bernhardt while she was playing *Hamlet* in London.

A French friend who knew her well took me to her.

Poor Sarah came dashing off the stage, looking like nothing on earth in Hamlet's dress, quite exhausted by her effort—a marvellous one for a woman of her age.

Her grace and kindness were superb, though we did not get very far in conversation, my French leaving much to be desired, and all her available English being "Tank you." I remember her so vividly now! Hers was a personality which extinguished every one else. My French friend *said* that the coffin she was reported to carry about with her was present in the dressing-room, but I can't honestly say I saw it. What I certainly saw was a large and terrifying bloodhound sitting bolt upright in an easy-chair.

A quaint little tale about these French friends recurs. They had two children, the typical French pigeon pair. When a third one was threatened, they sent in consternation for Dr. Burnett Smith. They did not want it and were in despair.

It duly arrived, however, a lovely baby, and when I congratulated the father, all he said was, with the inimitable French shrug and jerk of the fingers :

" Ah, oui, Madame, peut-être, mais elle n'est pas nécessaire ! "

One more vignette and I must hasten on, for there is yet much to tell.

Somebody conceived the idea of a hundred

distinguished women giving a party to a hundred distinguished men at the Grafton Galleries. It was a tremendous success. All sorts of unapproachable lions were lured from their dens, even Meredith and Hardy, and others of that ilk. Never, possibly, had such a galaxy of stars blazed at one moment in the literary firmament.

Sir William Robertson Nicoll came as my guest, and in the middle of the show he said, quite suddenly, with a queer, far-away look in his eyes :

" How many, do you suppose, in this gathering will be remembered in a hundred years ? "

I cast a startled glance round and shook my head.

" Only one," he said, in a sepulchral voice, pointing to Thomas Hardy.

CHAPTER TEN

HERTFORD DAYS

WE were twelve years in Hampstead, and left it in 1908, thus closing the vivid chapter of our London life.

The reasons for leaving London were at least sensible, though none of our friends seemed able to grasp them.

" Why," they asked, " should you leave a place where you have so many friends, where you are fully established, and drift out into the unknown, where anything may happen—even failure ? "

We listened, but did not falter, for we had, as we imagined, counted the cost. Our children were growing up, costing more and more for education every year ; their future and their careers had to be considered, and we were spending too much. We had got into a social set which could spend unlimited money, and we found it difficult to retrench or lay by anything for the rainy day. We lived in a large house, which required at least four servants to run, had a carriage, and generally lived the life of the well-to-do. So long as we were both working, we could keep it up, but once the personal element failed there was nothing behind it.

We went into, not one, but many committees of ways and means, and decided to sell out both house and practice and go into the country to live. It would be easy to find another practice, and by this cutting ourselves off from the old crowd we should be able to order our lives on a simpler basis.

It was a great wrench, of course. We knew it would be. It meant severing dear associations and parting with many loved friends. They were hard and difficult months while this new project was maturing, and both tempers and nerves were frayed. Effie was then at school in Lausanne, and the boy at the preparatory school at Durnford, Swanage, getting ready for Rugby.

Both house and practice were sold, dropping money, of course, by the transaction, as usual, then began the hunt for a new home. We stored the furniture, went to Kinghorn for a brief interlude, then the search began in earnest. We did not want to go too far from London, and my husband heard of a death vacancy in the county town of Hertford, about twenty miles out of London.

Satisfied with the particulars, he made the deal. I was still in Scotland and did not know very much about the transaction until it was put through. It was his affair, and I knew he would weigh it up well. I don't remember making any inquiry about the house in which we should have to live, and when I saw it, I confess I got a nasty jar. It was a mean and conspicuously ugly brick house on the street, small rooms, some of them dark, no indoor conveniences, and in a poor state of repair. Seeing my blank looks, Jim said :

" Never mind. Of course we shan't stop long in this house. It will be quite easy to get another after we've got established."

He didn't know, any more than I did, what he was talking about. There was no choice of houses in that old feudal town. They simply passed on from father to son, world without end, and the building craze had not then reached that backwater.

We moved in. I did my best to improve the house and make a home of it, but we all loathed it, even the children, who had been used to spacious rooms and a fine garden, in London. My husband was perfectly happy in his work. It was the same kind of work, with far more scope for surgery than ever falls to the lot of the general practitioner in London. He did not know how badly I was hit. It was my business to keep it from him. But I sometimes cried myself to sleep for all I had given up—for what ?

I will try to describe how drastic was the change. It was not a mere exchange from the city to the country. That I could have born cheerfully, having been originally a country bird and therefore having no illusions about country life. It was something far deeper and more searching than that. In Musselburgh we had sampled the individual flavour of the country town, but only in a very minor degree. There were no feudal conditions there such as had continued in Hertford since mediæval days. For me it a little resembled exchanging a rich feast, temptingly spread, for a dinner of herbs. It was well that love was not lacking, and it stood the test.

One curious feature of life in a country town is that those who come in from the outside are kept there, and though they may be kindly treated, they are never really considered to " belong " by the natives. This is no bad thing, nay, it is good, because it preserves the national flavour, but it can provide pretty cold comfort for those who, like us, desired to establish friendly relations and make a new home within the carefully guarded portals.

The county town possesses even more exclusive features. Most of the county business has to be done there, all the local interests converge upon it, and the Assizes, held there three or four times a year give it a picturesque, old-world flavour.

The Judge came in state to his " lodgings," generally found for him in one of the best-appointed houses in the neighbourhood, which the occupier must vacate, when desired to do so by the august majesty of the Law. He is amply compensated, but, I believe, has not the right to refuse.

The Assizes are opened by a state procession and service in the parish church, which the Mayor and Corporation have to attend in full robes. The Judge's coach, with its gay outriders and its herald, in company with the High Sheriff, makes quite an imposing picture and a nice splash of colour about the old streets adjacent to the Shire Hall. Only important cases, murders and such-like, are tried at the Assizes, and in our time many famous judges, Lord Alverstoke among them, were on circuit there.

I remember he sent me a message by his Marshal, the Hon. Alexander Shaw, who was our guest at the time, that if I put him in a novel as an unjust judge he would have me up for libel.

We had often smiled at the social cliques in Musselburgh, but they were totally eclipsed in the English county town, where the lines of demarcation were rigidly drawn. County did not mix with town, professional people with shopkeepers, church with chapel, and so on, through all the minor grades. It was rather a shock to me to find that in some mysterious fashion we seemed to have lost caste, and had no clearly defined social position, if any at all.

I heard a Hertford woman say one day : " It is a pity one can't know doctors socially. Some of them are really quite nice."

Another is reported to have said, though it was not in my hearing : " One doesn't receive doctors or solicitors, one sends for them." It was a nice distinction.

As for a woman who wrote books or spoke at meetings, she was a freak.

I am sure it was all quite excellent for me, and if I had ever had any tendency towards that strange disease called " swelled head," I ought to have been

drastically cured. After a time I could laugh and
extract the maximum of fun out of it. What a
priceless gift is the ability to see the queer side of
things ! It can carry one through the darkest day.

Of course, Hertford knew nothing about us, how
many doors had opened wide to us in London, nor
how many members of the class they worshipped
had sat with apparent happiness at our table. It
was not my concern to acquaint them with these
facts. They learned them for themselves as time
went by.

The " County," the predominant and overweening
influence governing social affairs, and from whose
judgment there was no appeal, afforded me a very
rich field for study. There was no end to it ; its
height, depth, and magnitude beggars description.
Landed estates, traditions, and ancient names
headed the hierarchy, though, later, money began to
pull its weight. It was very intriguing to watch the
gradual evolution of the successful moneymaker
into the county magnate. Hertfordshire, one of the
most exclusive residential counties in England,
abounded in such examples of successful climbing.
The place was full of climbers who meekly accepted
innumerable snubs, amply recompensed, if permitted
to bask occasionally in exalted smiles.

After the delightful social atmosphere from which
we had come, this seemed a strange, new, impossible world. It did not affect my husband in the
least. He just laughed at it, and was so happy,
building up his practice among people who loved

and appreciated him, that he had no regrets. Nor had I really ; the daily shocks I received acted as a tonic. Then I had my work. Without it, possibly I might have perished.

We had left, among other things, a very happy church connection at St. Andrew's, Frognal, which, as members of the Scots Colony in Hampstead, we had helped to build. We found a new home in another St. Andrew's, the parish church across the road, and the Rector and his wife became our friends. But he died not very long after we arrived, and his successor, discovering that we were Presbyterians and had never been confirmed, sadly but firmly informed us that we must not attend Communion. He suggested a private confirmation service at St. Paul's in London, but I indignantly refused.

Always impulsive and eager to get at the heart of things, I went up to the Rectory to ask the Rector where in the Bible he could find the mandate for what he had done. It was a quite futile interview. All he said of a definite nature was that he had written to the Bishop of St. Albans, the head of the diocese. I ought to have written to him myself, or gone to see him. Afterwards, when I got to know him, I was sorry I had not. During my husband's Mayoralty he was frequently a guest in our house, and was one of the most delightful we had ever entertained. His answer to our Rector's query was very guarded, its substance being that it is not wise to disturb existing communions.

8

I felt inclined to leave St. Andrew's Church, but my husband, less impulsive, and certainly wiser about many things, decided that we should carry on, and make no difference, except in abstaining from the Communion.

But I missed those quiet early morning services, which seemed to bring one so near to the unseen, and I used to get on my bicycle and run out to Waterford where, in the little village church, was a vicar of Christ who saw things differently.

About two years later, the Rector invited us to return to his Communion. I never understood the logic of that gesture, but we accepted the olive branch. One cannot but think that such narrow sectarianism must do much harm to the cause of religion.

While we were wrestling with these various problems, and finding our feet, so to speak, in our new home, Destiny was marching on, bringing us to 1910—one of the most disastrous years of our life.

We had had a wonderful holiday in Scotland with the children, partly at Kinghorn and partly at our old haunt Amulree, where father and son had long golden days with basket and rod on the burns and the lochs. They were inseparable companions, never was there a cloud between them. Ned told his father everything about his work, his games, and the problems which beset schoolboy life.

There comes a time in her son's life when the mother has to stand by, when he does not need

EDWARD BURNETT SMITH. AGED 15
DIED 1910

her as in his childhood. If his father fails him then, why, the loss to both is irremediable. Thank God my son's father did not fail him.

We came home as usual early in September, to prepare for the new school term. He had then been a year at Rugby. It was the last day of the holidays, and he was putting all his things in order to leave them behind till Christmas. He had put his golf sticks in the bag, and at the last tried to push in a small rifle his father had brought him from America.

Apparently a charge had been left in it.

From the hall there reached me in the drawing-room a sudden sharp report. I rushed out, to find him lying face downwards on the rug.

He only lived half an hour.

The tragedy for us, who had built such high hopes on him, is summed up in the words of Job, inscribed on the cross which stands in the windy hill at Kinghorn :

" My purposes are broken off."

CHAPTER ELEVEN

SPIRITUALISM

THE bereavement which quenches the loveliest of human hopes is the supreme test of religious faith. It is women who meet it with courage and resource. Men—such gallant fighters among material things or for great causes—are like frightened children when the citadel of life is shaken.

My husband, usually so strong and calm and independent, collapsed utterly, and I was so anxious about him I had to crush down my own sorrow and stand by for any emergency.

The bond between that particular father and son was very close and rare. To the boy his father was the buttress of the universe. He told him everything—all his childish troubles, his schoolboy scrapes, the problems of the adolescent years. When I was going through his things later, I found a packet of his father's letters, written through the whole period of his school life. Glancing through them—amazed at their wisdom and tenderness and understanding of the boy's soul—I felt that there was a side of the man I had married which I knew nothing about.

His anguish was frightful, and accentuated by the fact that he had bought him the gun and taught him to use it.

It was no comfort at all to him to be reminded of the other Home to which, for some mysterious reason, the boy had been summoned in the spring-time of his days. I remember trying to comfort him with these exquisite lines of R. L. S. :

" All that life contains of torture, toil, and treason,
   Shame, dishonour, death were but a name.
Here, a boy, he dwelt through all the singing season,
   And ere the day of sorrow departed as he came."

It was no use. It was many weeks before he could speak rationally about it, and his heart never recovered really from that mortal blow.

We took the dear body to Kinghorn, travelling by night, a ghastly journey. His poor father wanted to go and sit beside the casket in the dark, remembering how the child had feared the dark all his life.

We laid him to rest by the sea in the heavenly calm of a perfect autumn day, in presence of a great company of mourners, who had come from all parts uninvited to show their sympathy. The townspeople, who had known and loved him since his babyhood, closed their shop doors and drew down the blinds to follow the simple funeral train. All the clan had gathered from far and near, a large and comforting company.

Effie, so still and self-contained, spoke but little after the one despairing cry. In a few days all was over, and we had to go back without him to the waiting duty.

Precious were the letters we received, especially from Rugby, from his House Master, and from the Head, Mr. David, now Bishop of Liverpool, who wrote that, from inquiry, he had learned that very few in so short a time had established such a fine, clean, lovable record. I believe that there are born into the world a certain number of the flawlessly pure in heart, whom the world, the flesh, and the devil are powerless to smirch. He was one of these. And perhaps God, knowing how acute would be his suffering later on, took him without ado into the higher life.

This theory, so very comforting to me, was no use at all to his father, who rejected it to the last day of his own life.

It did not occur to us to leave the scene of our bitter sorrow. We were dumb in the face of it, all our old restlessness stilled. Our fellow-townsmen and women were extraordinarily kind to us, showing us a warm sympathy which not only helped at the time but laid the foundations of many lasting friendships. When once the barriers are down, human nature is much the same everywhere and in all classes. Humanity is stronger than caste.

There were, however, some whom I shall describe as the misunderstanding ones.

Remembering the warning couplet :

> " Laugh, and the world laughs with you.
> Weep, and you weep alone,"

I was doing my best to present a brave face. One day, in Fore Street, I met a woman who remarked cheerfully :

" How nice that you have got over it so quickly ! "

I remember just getting out " Yes, isn't it ? " before I staggered on, biting my lips and striving to keep back the tears. Was I, then, disloyal to his precious memory ? Perish the thought !

As time went on, I felt myself more and more drawn towards contemplation of the Heavenly City which, after my son's death, became at times more real and dear than any on earth. Then again would come spells of depression and doubt, when all seemed remote, shadowy, and impossible, and uppermost would surge the searching question, " What if death ends all, and he is lost for ever ? "

It was in one of these moods common to all mourners that I was tempted to inquire whether spiritualism had anything to offer in the way of consolation. I happened to have a Scotch friend, Mrs. Duffus, one of our neighbours in Hampstead, who, bereaved of her husband and one of her children, professed to have found amazing comfort in spiritualism and to have established contact with the other side.

My husband was not keen about this, but he offered no strenuous objections when she urged me to attend a séance with her at the house of one Husk, a blind medium, in whom my old friend, W. T. Stead, one of the earliest and most fervent devotees of spiritualism, had had profound faith.

At that séance there were certainly some happenings both strange and inexplicable, but no comfort came to me. Strange faces materialised, some of them even familiar, and all sorts of voices came through, one of them purporting to be my son's.

But it conveyed no message to my aching heart, and I resented with my whole soul the idea of glorified spirits making themselves known in such trivial, even vulgar, fashion through such queer avenues of communication. Possibly I was a hostile sitter, though I imagined I had gone with an open mind.

I afterwards recorded my impressions in the *Woman at Home*, which attracted some attention and provoked some rather lively correspondence between me and Mr. W. T. Stead. He sent me a copy of his *Letters from Julia*. I fear they left me cold.

Some years later, while the war was in progress and there were so many Rachels mourning for their sons and refusing to be comforted, Mrs. Duffus persuaded me to accompany her to a sitting with a famous trumpet medium from America called Mrs. Wreibt. We had a private sitting with her one morning at her flat in Kensington. I found her a very sweet, spirituelle little woman, the very last you would associate with any sort of fraud. The experience was certainly odd.

The three of us sat in a small, dark room, with bare walls and only one door, entirely empty except for a trumpet on the floor, the three chairs ranged round it. There was no touching of hands, no sort of physical contact at all. We talked, because Mrs. Wreibt said that talking helped what she called the vibrations. Suddenly there was a rustling sound in the trumpet, and presently a very deep, raucous man's voice boomed out, addressing me by name.

It was Stead's voice, easily recognisable by any one who had known him. He had not long passed over in the appalling disaster of the *Titanic*. The medium became very agitated, while Stead and I held a more or less animated conversation. He informed me that the entire resources of the spirit world were being concentrated on the conduct of the war, and that there was much " sorting out," as he described it, of the thousands of souls, many of them elemental, passing over every day. He also said that at the moment they were actively circumventing the German invasion of England, which had actually materialised. Asked how long the war would last, he said he could not tell, but that the Allies would win.

At that same sitting my grandfather and grand-mother also paid me a visit, and most certainly the intimate family affairs, some of which I had entirely forgotten, could not possibly have been known either to the medium or to Mrs. Duffus. Nor were they in my mind.

A low, soft voice, purporting to be my son's, assured me that he was never absent from my side, more especially when I was in my study in the early, quiet morning hours.

I must not forget to say that just before this voice spoke, Mrs. Wreibt said quite suddenly :

" I see a tall figure in grey beside Mrs. Smith's chair. He has a large ginger cat with a broad face and big eyes in his arms, and at his feet a little, low grey dog with an appealing face."

Both these creatures, a magnificant tabby cat and a Skye terrier, given to us by the Leightons, had died the same year as the boy. They were great pets of his.

I have no explanation of these things to offer. That it all happened is undeniable, for I took copious notes at the time.

I seem to have got into touch at the time with Sir Oliver Lodge, for I find this letter :

" DEAR MRS. BURNETT SMITH.—I cannot help thinking you have an exaggerated idea of the harm that may have been done to feeble-minded folk by Spiritualism. It is difficult to be sure how much is cause and how much effect.

" I know that there are people whom it is well to warn off the subject. But I expect most of them will come to grief or get foolish in some other way. I also know that there are a large number of bereaved people who have derived comfort, and whose religious faith has been strengthened by the information which psychical science is able to bring to them, whether they deal with it first or second hand.

" However, I need not enlarge on that aspect of

the subject beyond asking people of authority, like yourself, to be careful how they condemn any branch of the truth, for they may thereby be taking too much responsibility upon themselves.

" Every real truth must have its divine aspect. Inattention to that aspect may be pardonable, but indiscriminate abuse of it may verge perilously near to blasphemy.

" However, now I am merely talking generalities and am not thinking of any individual case.

" With very kind regards.—Faithfully yours,
" OLIVER LODGE."

About that time there was a very venomous attack in the *Daily Mail* on Sir Oliver's book *Raymond*. For some strange reason the article or review, which I did not even see, was attributed to me ; and I wrote to J. Arthur Hill, denying it. He replied :

" DEAR MRS. BURNETT SMITH,—I am indeed glad to have your letter. The thought of you having apparently written that thing in the *Daily Mail* bothered us a good deal, for the vulgar and lying article seemed quite out of keeping with what I knew of you through your work. I hope you have read *Raymond*, and did not take your idea of it from the *Daily Mail* travesty.

" I agree emphatically, and so does Sir Oliver, that psychical investigation is not for everybody. Neither is anatomy. In many sciences there are unpleasant features which tend to upset stomachs or weak minds, and it is perhaps specially so in psychical research. We often dissuade people from seeking personal experience. I do it very strongly in my book *Psychical Investigation*.

"Of course it is no substitute for religion. That is a bigger thing. I join with you heartily in detesting 'occultism,' palmistry, and the fashionable superstitions of the West End. Psychical research is a serious study, best left, as far as possible, to specialists, though ordinary, well-balanced people, properly guided, and not left to consult mediums indiscriminately, may and do often get great comfort and no harm from it.

"With friendly regards.—Yours sincerely,
"J. ARTHUR HILL."

For many years I left the matter alone and had no further excursions into the realm of psychical inquiry, though my interest in it continued lively. I have had opportunities within the last few years of meeting Sir Oliver Lodge, and have had several talks with him in my own house. I imagined him, though not less confident in his belief in survival after death, and the possibility of communicating with those who have passed over, somewhat vague about the tangible results of psychic research. They are always more or less shadowy, and many gaps and discrepancies have to be left to faith and imagination.

Not long ago I was persuaded by some very sincere

and respected friends to attend a sitting in Edinburgh again. I was disappointed, and can only record the fact that, according to my very partial judgment, very little advance seemed to have been made.

Of course much must depend on the sitter. I was never hostile, but possibly too casual and not open-minded enough.

There have, however, been marvellous and undoubted developments in other directions, notably that of automatic writing, which is quite independent of dark rooms and favourable vibrations. I had the privilege lately of spending a couple of hours in London with Miss Geraldine Cummins, the author of two books, *The Great Days of Ephesus*, and *The Road to Immortality*, which she has written automatically under trance conditions to the dictation of the late F. H. W. Myers. She had a message for me during that sitting, the accuracy of which I could not gainsay.

I have, of course, never doubted for a moment, nor questioned, the great theory of survival after death. Acceptance of it is part of the faith in which I was reared, and which has never failed me, through all the vicissitudes and hazards of a long and strenuous life.

As regards spiritualism, however, I am bound to record that, so far as clearing up the mysteries of life and death is concerned, I have found no road that way.

CHAPTER TWELVE

MORE HERTFORD DAYS

IT never occurred to us to leave the scene of our bitter sorrow. We were dumb before it, all our restlessness stilled. We slogged away, with a detached interest, at our work until new interests and claims began to change the outlook. That is the law of life. If it were not so, then it would be good-bye to progress and a drastic limit set to human effort.

The first thing which lifted us clean out of the groove into which we had sunk was the offer of the Mayoralty to the Doctor after a year or two of active and popular service on the Town Council.

The civic life of the provincial town has from time immemorial provided a rich mine for the caricaturist, its humours being a godsend to the comic papers. It has survived all that, and will survive, because it is an integral part of the British Constitution.

The English civic system differs in some of its features from that which pertains to Scotland. The Mayor's term of office is yearly, and when it ends he remains a member of the Council, with a chance of being elected again, if he desires it, to the mayoral chair. There were good citizens in Hertford who had served three or four mayoral terms. My husband was elected twice.

In Scotland, when the Provost retires at the end of the third year, he officially retires and is exempt from any further Corporation service. Many good public servants have assured me that the change is too drastic, and that they found it difficult to adjust their compasses in consequence. I suppose the system has something to recommend it. At least it gives younger men a chance. A Mayor or a Provost finds that he has very little time for his private business during his term of office. That so many men are willing to sacrifice a good deal in this way says much for their public spirit. Of course there are compensations. Most men enjoy the sense of power it confers as well as the honour. To be trusted by your fellow-citizens is a satisfying thing.

Our particular Mayor had a hard time of it, trying to overtake continuous public work in conjunction with a large and ever-increasing practice. His working day was seldom shorter than sixteen hours. An eight-hour day had no meaning for him.

I was able to help him in a very minor degree, opening sales of work and such like, where my years of platform experience proved useful. The Mayor himself became an excellent speaker through practice, and the number of " causes " of which he had to acquire a slight working knowledge was legion. It was a very happy year, in which there were two outstanding events.

The Marquis of Salisbury is the over-lord of Hertford, owning much property in the town, including the picturesque Hertford Castle, a relic of mediæval times. He offered the Castle and grounds to the town, and it was a great occasion when the gift was handed over by Lord and Lady Salisbury in person. It was a lovely day. We had a big luncheon party at the Shire Hall, attended by the Lord Lieutenant and all the county magnates. The public turned out in full force to acclaim the generous donors, and next day all our pictures were in the papers. We also went in state to see ourselves on the screen at the local cinema.

The Castle, right in the middle of the town, has been an enormous and much-appreciated boon, the building serving to house many Corporation depart-ments, while the grounds provide a very pretty public park.

Hatfield is only seven miles distant from Hert-ford, and the Salisburys took a deep interest in the town. Some of the conditions under which pro-perty could be acquired and used seemed to me to savour of feudal times, and many of the later incomers commented on it. But on the whole the relations were of the happiest description.

The county town was long a backwater, served by the Great Eastern Railway, also by a little train, running between it and Hatfield Junction. Travelling by that train round the vast and difficult unnecessary curve ordained by a former Marquis, when the line was laid down, in order that the amenity of the Hatfield woods might not be even remotely threatened, raised in one's mind considerable questioning.

We were fortunate, during our first mayoral year, to acquire a new habitation, which we had often coveted. The North House was an old Georgian house of no particular merit, but the garden was lovely, offering tempting facilities for the fêtes and garden parties which are so much a feature of country life. There were five acres of lawns, and wood, and meadow, intersected by a tributary of the Lea, which created enchanting vistas. An old, picturesque bridge spanned it at one part ; under it a deep pool where enormous speckled trout, as old as the house, I believe, played about lazily. They lured many anglers, but only experts were successful. One requires to know the secrets of these sluggish English streams, which bear no resemblance to the dancing, singing burns of the north country. They are silent, contemplative waters, by which one could sit and dream for hours, but they are not rich in surprises or ecstatic thrills. The trout were firm and pink-fleshed, but we could not eat them, owing to their queer, muddy flavour.

We gave a great garden party that summer, on a perfect day, receiving all sorts and conditions, including many of our London friends, who motored down and were delighted, as well as surprised, to find us in such attractive surroundings. Our life

9

was full of kaleidoscopic effects, and I had opportunities to study human nature under many auspices.
I was, however, never tempted to write a novel
about Hertford. Loyalty to the people and the
place that had been so good to us forbade it. Frank
Swinnerton wrote one called *Shops and Houses*,
which we all greatly enjoyed. It was not written
about our town, though it might have been.

In comparison with the more privileged male,
who could "arise and go to Innisfree," or anywhere
else he liked, in search of fresh material, the women
writers of my day worked under a handicap, being
expected to stop at home, and not encouraged to
make themselves conspicuous in any way. All is
changed now. But even then there were a few
adventurous souls, who fared forth into the unknown, defying every kind of convention. Among
them were Mary Kingsley, an intrepid and very
able explorer, and Mary Gaunt, both of whom I
knew well.

I remember Miss Gaunt making my flesh creep
with a very circumstantial account of a trek she
took through a primeval, virgin forest, attended
only by her native bearer. Physical courage having
been left out of my composition, such a feat would
have been impossible for me. I am even afraid of
the friendly dark.

My life certainly provided sufficient movement
and colour to satisfy a modest pen.

Effie "came out" that year, at the Hatfield
Ball, by invitation of Lady Salisbury. The Hat-

EFFIE   1914

field Ball was the great event of the season, only
exceeding in importance the Hertford County Ball.

The County Ball occasioned many heart-burnings
among the climbers, who pestered the lives of the
members of the selection committee, who sent out
the invitations.   There was a legend that, so rigidly
were the lines drawn, that the company was divided
into two sections—those who had the right to step
on the carpet before the dais, and the other sort.
The first time I attended, the carpet was naturally
an object of great interest to me, but I soon saw
that the legend, like many others, only existed in the
imagination.   It was a delightful, brilliant affair,
the red coats of the hunting contingent making a
bright splash of colour.

Hatfield is one of the treasure-houses of England,
as well as of unrivalled historic interest.   Its hospitality at all times was worthy of its setting and
tradition.   We were guests in London at the wedding
of Lady Beatrice Cecil who married Mr. Ormesby
Gore.   I remember seeing on the stairs at Arlington
Street that day Lord David Cecil, later the accomplished author of *The Stricken Deer*.   He was then a
sunny-faced little boy, looking very attractive in his
page's suit.

I took Effie to Court during her father's year of
office, and I fear I took a mildly malicious delight
in the local sensation it created.   I had never
breathed a word about any social success I had had
in London, but accepted quite meekly, outwardly at
least, the verdict of my new neighbours.   If my

position in Hertford, or anywhere indeed, had depended on the tactics of the wire-pulling climbers, I should have remained in happy obscurity for ever.

One day I was travelling to London on our little train with one of the local ladies, who had been at some pains to show me my place. She was always polite, of course, from a great height. We talked a little of local affairs, and I mentioned casually that I was going to the dressmaker.

" You don't get things made in Hertford then ? " she said. " S. & B. have quite a good woman, I believe."

I replied that I knew they had, but this was rather special, a Court frock, in fact.

" Oh, for whom, might I inquire ? " she asked, her eyes beginning to glow.

I told her I was presenting my daughter at the June Court.

She sat forward, as if to challenge my statement, then said " Oh ! " with a kind of snort, and opened out her *Times*. She had never been to Court, though her life was largely spent in cultivating and paying court to the great ones of the earth.

But are they the great ones ? The accident of birth does not necessarily confer greatness.

These may seem trivial happenings to include in my life-story, but they were all part of its web, besides being great fun.

There were many delightful strands in the Hertford web. Among the true friends who enriched my life there were two women of the same name, though they were in no way related.

I was deeply interested when I learned that Mrs. Florence Barclay, author of *The Rosary* and many other books which achieved phenomenal popularity on both sides of the Atlantic, was the wife of the vicar of Hertford Heath, up on the lovely hilltop where Haileybury College, with all its young, gay life, brightens the picturesque landscape.

It was some little time before I met her, for she did not call on me when we arrived to take up our abode in Hertford. I should not imagine that she was a " calling " person, being unconventional in all her ways. She was very unlike her books. There was not a suggestion of mushy sentimentality about the sturdy little figure in homespun, crowned by a queer sort of velvet hat, a cross between a beret and a Scotch cap, without which she was never seen. She had a vivid, interesting face and a pair of intense, flashing dark eyes, which lit it up in a quite marvellous way. Also she had a very deep, rich voice, which must have been most effective on public platforms, though I never heard her there. I don't think she did very much public speaking, certainly she did not spend herself as I did on a thousand infinitesimal things.

I always felt that little, struggling causes, fighting against odds, sometimes in obscure corners, were more in need of help than more spectacular ones. So I made tremendous journeys to open obscure little sales of work or speak to a handful of women, without ever pausing to count the cost. Whatever that cost was, it has been paid in full by the gratitude and affection of those I tried to serve. Mrs. Barclay concentrated more. She had a marvellous Men's Bible Class at Hertford Heath which had a reputation far beyond its native heath.

She was an extraordinary and very brilliant woman, and her eyes could fascinate you. She wrote her books in a little house built in the Vicarage garden, or rather in a field just beyond it, and nobody was allowed to disturb her there, or enter without permission. When she showed me that little hermitage, which held all her books and papers, on which she could lock the door, I was aware of a slight pang of envy. Surely it would be easier to do better, more enduring work in such a sanctuary, cut off from everything that could interrupt or disturb one's thoughts ? Such luxury had never been possible for me. At Mountskip I wrote a lot of stuff in old copy-books, sitting on the "fender end" in the kitchen, and I was quite a mature matron before I achieved a study, my work being done in holes and corners, though never at the fag end of the day.

I remember being filled with awe when Max Pemberton's wife told me the household had to creep about like mice in case any possible sound should reach the study.

I don't think anybody has the right to keep other people in bondage like that. Obviously the solution is a little lodge in the wilderness like Florence

Barclay's, or an office rented outside, at a safe distance from one's home.

Marie Corelli had different sanctuaries in her lovely garden at Mason Croft to which she retired with her changing moods. One mysterious "howff" was a little house in a tree to which she climbed by a ladder.

Perhaps I might have done better work had I been able to shut out the world like that, but all my days I have been accessible, even during my working hours, to the butcher, the baker, and the candlestick maker.

Florence Barclay was an understanding creature. Being the mother of ten children, she had acquired wisdom in a very well-equipped school. I find her writing sympathisingly to me on many occasions. I had several letters from her in the Nursing Home at Harrogate. In one these sentences occur :

" I am glad that dear brave heart went on beating. I, for one, would feel the world sadly poorer without it. I am sure that the sense of discouragement and uselessness you speak of was brought about by this illness being on the way, and also through giving out so much in your splendid war service. You have had so much to bear of shocks and loss, giving yourself all the while, that I am glad indeed to hear that a period of complete rest is enjoined by those in authority."

Again :

" When are you coming to the Temple again ? I hardly know how to wait.

" I loved your *Toovey* (a little dramatic sketch I wrote and presented at the Shire Hall in aid of some good cause). The golden heart is one and the same, whether it beats beneath a linen apron, with a brave black smut on the defiant nose, or whether it carries its owner, still simple, strong, and sweet, through the higher ranks of our great social life, or along the uncertain, thorny paths of our beloved literature."

To me she was always one of the encouragers, and I mourned sincerely over her untimely death.

The other friend, Mrs. Hubert Barclay, was a very different woman—beautiful, gracious, and wise—with a deeply spiritual nature and a most attractive personality.

She also was a writer of novels, but her best work, I think, was done in another realm. She was the President of the Mothers' Union, and did a tremendous lot of speaking for it during her presidential years. I have heard of her work in all sorts of unexpected quarters, and every one who met her was impressed by her charm, her insight, and her deep spiritual experience. She was a wonderful friend to me during the testing war years when I was often lonely and depressed. Her husband, Lieut.-Colonel Hubert Barclay, trained and commanded the Kitchener 6th Batt. Bedfordshire Regiment and took them to France.

I was all the while very busy with my creative work. I had contracts, chiefly with Messrs. Leng of Dundee (about whom I will write more fully later) and others, which kept me at work all the time. One of the secrets of amicable relations with editors is convincing them by experience that you are absolutely dependable. Some writers I know, especially of serial work, cause themselves and others unnecessary strain and irritation by never being up to time and giving no guarantee that they ever *will* be up to time. I could not live or work like that. I am an orderly person, and in the case of serial work, have always delivered the completed MSS. before it was due to be printed.

In addition I was then in the full tide of public work, speaking for various good causes in all parts of the country. When we left London, of course, some of the regular committee and other active work had to be given up, but I remained available for any special occasions.

Although public work has absorbed a tremendous amount of my time and strength, I have never regretted it. It has been of incalculable benefit to me in every way, enlarging my knowledge of many areas of human experience which I could not otherwise have reached.

From the day when the Founder of the Salvation Army startled the world with *In Darkest England*, I have been deeply interested in the work of the Army and served it in many ways. I wrote several books for them, describing the many-sided activities in which they have been so long and successfully engaged. I felt a strange thrill the night I marched by Mrs. Bramwell Booth's side down Regent Street, singing to the strains of the band, " Home, Sweet Home." We were a Salvage Corps that night, out to gather in some of the " daughters of joy " from the streets.

I have stood at the gates of Wandsworth Gaol in the chill of the very early morning, to get hold of the released prisoners and offer them a helping hand. I have talked with murderers and other kinds of criminals, whom the authorities had entrusted to the after-care of the Army, and I have found them mostly simple, rather pathetic souls.

Many of the major crimes for which men and women have to suffer either the death penalty, or life sentences, have been committed in a moment of blind, tempestuous passion, or under severe provocation. These are not in the same class with the fiendish crimes committed by sadistic persons, of whom the world is better rid. It requires a marvellous combination of intellect and intuition to shoulder such heavy responsibilities. But British justice is equal to the stupendous task.

Another great redemptive institution in which I have been deeply interested since its inception is the West Ham Central Mission, created and maintained by the marvellous, consecrated labours of Mr. and Mrs. Rowntree Clifford. This is only one of many such organisations operating in the depressed East End areas, but of its marvellous results I can speak with first-hand knowledge.

I sometimes wonder whether our country knows,

or rather, realises what it owes to all these devoted missioners of Christ. But for their wise ministry and self-denying effort, the fires of hate, and jealousy, and revenge for the unequal distribution, not of wealth alone, but even of the bare necessities of life, would undoubtedly flare up into one vast conflagration, in which civilisation might be engulfed and destroyed. Let the comfortable and the well-to-do, who shut their eyes to facts, and are cheerfully assured that it is quite a good world, not be chary of helping those who are bearing the burden " down east," and elsewhere, and so fulfil the law of Christ.

Let them rather dip deeply into their pockets and hand out generously. It may easily prove the best and safest investment they have ever made, in a world rocking on its very foundation.

CHAPTER THIRTEEN

THE WAR YEARS

I WAS in Scotland when war was declared. So far as I am aware, I have no Highland strain in me, but again and again I have been startled, sometimes disconcerted, by consciousness of a hidden power which has made me aware of things before they happened.

All that summer I was obsessed by a nameless fear. I was not then in political circles, and my only knowledge of current events, as affecting the international situation, was obtained from the newspapers. Like other members of an intelligent public, I was aware that things were not well in the Near East and that trouble was brewing in the Balkan States. Germany's preparedness for war was quite often the subject of speculation, and a good many jokes were passed about the Day.

So near and real were my fears, haunting me night and day, that I actually wrote an article for the *Woman at Home* on Fear, pointing out what a powerful factor it had been in the history of nations, as well as in the lives of private individuals. It contained no reference at all to current events, nor to the flying rumours in the air.

The last week in July I had travelled with the household by train, leaving the Doctor and Effie to come by road in a new car he had just given her. It was a Studebaker, a dashing little two-seater, painted a lovely blue. She was one of the first women motorists to be seen about the Hertfordshire lanes, and was very proud of her new treasure. Little did we anticipate the ultimate fate of our pretty blue Judy, nor how she would return to her base a shattered hulk, covered with the wounds of war.

They were on the road on August the fourth, and had some adventures, also much trouble about petrol, the entire supply of which was at once commandeered by the Government. The whole country was immediately thrown into an incredible state of panic, in which many foolish and unnecessary things were done.

They were late in arriving and considered themselves lucky to have got through with the car, as the authorities were seizing everything in the way of motor vehicles, sometimes causing the bereft serious inconvenience. Never, surely, did a country go into war so utterly unprepared.

We often laughed afterwards at the haste with which Effie drove her new possession up to Glassmount, where some friends offered to hide it in the barn. It was covered entirely over with hay and straw, until the panic had somewhat subsided.

I don't remember that we had any qualms about
this wicked deed. What use, anyway, would a
girl's dainty toy be in the war zone ? Later on,
however, it did its bit.

Kinghorn, I must explain, was one of the most
unpleasant of the Home Bases to live in during the
war. It had become—after we built our house—
one of the most important defences of the Forth.
Its proximity to the Forth Bridge and the Naval
Base at Rosyth made it of the first importance.
Greatly to our regret, year by year the defences
were strengthened, barbed wire appeared everywhere, and bigger and better guns were installed on
terrifying emplacements. The biggest of all was
not more than two hundred yards from our house,
the chief gunner's cottage intervening in the space
between.

The close proximity of the Fort entirely destroyed
the amenity of our property, and when the guns
were fired for practice our windows were regularly
shattered. For that there was no compensation.

Immediately the war broke out, Kinghorn became
a lively centre of military activity. Barriers were
erected across the road just outside our front gate,
in order to prevent any unauthorised persons from
approaching the Fort. Sentries were posted there
night and day, and there was no respite from the
challenge :

" Halt ! Who goes there ? Advance one, and
be recognised ! "

The panicky atmosphere of these first weeks was

indescribable. The bogey was German invasion, which was reported to be imminent, sometimes actually to have materialised, at every vulnerable spot along the coast. Trenches were dug and manned by night and day, vigilant watch kept everywhere, explicit instructions handed out to the civilians as to their procedure when the enemy actually arrived.

The whole of life was transformed into something grim and sinister. Our cellars were commandeered for the Red Cross stores, so that they would be quickly available when the fighting began. It was, of course, necessary to keep vigilant watch over the narrow channel leading to the Forth Bridge, which the enemy were anxious to blow up, in order to block the outlet for the Fleet at the Rosyth Base.

All the little islands we so loved and had often picnicked on became armed camps ; the sea, a menacing highway on which anything might happen. The scares were continuous and exciting. One day it was reported that the Germans had actually effected a landing at Largo Bay, and I have to confess that I was so scared that I ran away, making a hasty trip by rail to the old Manse at Lumsden, where the Nicolls were enjoying a peaceful holiday. It restored my shattered nerves for a little, and I was grateful for the interlude, though I had to stand a good deal of chaff when I got home. I didn't mind. I have never pretended that physical courage was my strong suit.

Effie and her father were quite unperturbed.

They had no fear of an invading army, and were quite thoroughly enjoying all the unheard-of excitement.

There is no doubt that a good many lost their heads during these early days. Small wonder, as Lloyd George truly said, " For peace-loving countries war is an undiscovered country through which a pathway has yet to be found."

Funny things happened. One day there arrived at our gate a small military contingent with a quantity of boards and tools to deal therewith, informing me that their instructions were to board up the bathroom window, as it overlooked the Fort. My husband arrived on the scene and made short work of them, ordering them off, as he had no intention whatever of allowing his bathroom window to be boarded up. They departed meekly, though evidently surprised. Of course we knew the matter could not end there, so after consulting together, he made a happy suggestion that we should invite the Military Governor and his aide-de-camp to become guests in our house. We knew they had not got comfortable quarters, as there was no good hotel in the place. The invitation was duly conveyed and gladly accepted, and we heard no more about boarding up the bathroom window.

They were delightful guests and gave me a certain sense of security, though I never got used to the telephone bell from the Fort ringing suddenly in the middle of the night, or men rushing along the paved passage to the front door, opening it—for it was never allowed to be locked—and dashing up to the Governor's room. Then we would hear a hurried colloquy, and presently the Governor and his aide dashing down the stairs. Of course we never heard anything about the scares. Our job was to endure. I remember one day Major Baker Kerr, the aide, who was rather amused at my nervous fears, showed me a German paper in which it was quite seriously reported that Kinghorn Fort had been destroyed and Edinburgh bombarded. That was the sort of stuff the German public was fed on. I suppose they needed it to keep up their blind faith in their military and naval strength. Altogether it could not be said that we had a restful holiday, and we were all quite glad, I think, for the first time, to leave our loved kingdom by the sea and return to the comparative peace of Hertford.

The only way those on the Home Front could endure the stress of these times was by plunging into whatever activities were available to absorb their energies and make them feel that they were helping a little. We found that all sorts of work had sprung into being, Red Cross Depots, where anxious and willing women spent hours rolling bandages and preparing comforts for the wounded, already, alas! taxing hospital accommodation everywhere. That sort of work did not appeal much to me. I could not sit still long enough. I had the gift of speech, and it was not long before I was using it in the training camps, both in England and Scotland.

10

I wish I could set down here some of the glory and heartbreak of it all. These were the Crusaders, young, pure, and high-hearted. Never had the world seen such an army, nor ever will again. The great majority sleep—their precious dust, at least—on the fields of France and Flanders, but their souls are marching on.

Of course I was anxious to get out to France, and it was not long before the opportunity came through the Y.M.C.A., for whom I had already done much work in the home camps, also at the munition factories.

I was allowed to take Effie with me, though the censorship of unauthorised visitors to France was strictly enforced, the authorities being determined that there should be no repetition of the plague of useless women of whom Kitchener complained during the Boer War. Effie's proficiency in the French language paved the way, and soon we were on our way from Southampton to Havre, the longer sea-route being considered rather safer than the much-menaced Channel passage.

The picturesque old French seaport had been transformed out of all knowledge into a base camp of huge dimensions, with all the accompaniments inseparable from active service. It was early summer then, and the public gardens presented a most amazing spectacle which must have filled the natives with wonder. Every nationality and all colours seemed to be taking the air there of an afternoon, the sober khaki of the British and the bluish-grey of the French troops, splashed with the colours from the East. It was chiefly at Havre that the constantly reinforced army was sifted and partly trained, and the camp at Honfleur was a sight to see.

I started in to work at once, speaking in the huts every night. It was a message of gratitude and encouragement from the women at home I was charged with, as well as the burden of deeper things, and how joyfully they received it ! For these young recruits were all Crusaders still, eager and undismayed, because convinced of the righteousness of their cause. The little services were good, but for me the best part of the work was the " forgathering " at the close, when we talked face to face, they telling me all about their homes, showing me pictures of their mothers, wives, bairns, sweethearts, and sisters. I took down sheaves of addresses and did my best to write to all their dear ones when I got home, but as time went on, the task became gargantuan, and had to be abandoned.

The devotion and efficiency of the Y.M.C.A. workers were marvellous. There was no side of the men's life and experience they did not try to reach, generally with conspicuous success. One day the Superintendent asked me whether I would go and speak to the men in a concentration camp some way outside the town. Not having the faintest idea what a concentration camp was, I said cheerfully : " Of course I will ! " When he came to fetch me from our lodging, I thought he looked rather oddly at Effie, then said : " Oh, well, we can leave her in the car."

I sat in front with him, and on the way he enlightened me about the nature of the concentration camp, where over a thousand men and lads were segregated from their comrades, having contracted venereal disease. It was a great shock to me, and I could not imagine what I could find to say to them. However, having put my hand to the plough, there was no turning back, but it was a poignant moment when I, a woman, alone, faced them on that sunny hillside to offer them my message. It is marvellous how one is helped in such moments of stress. I have never known it to fail. I found words, beholding in them the menfolk of praying and anxious women at home. But it shook me a little. It was my first introduction to one of the minor horrors of war.

From Havre we passed on to Rouen, most beautiful of the little cities on the Seine. We had some marvellous days there, and felt ourselves getting nearer what was loosely referred to as the Front. It was when we left the cheerful atmosphere of the towns and went to remote places that I had some qualms of fear. Without Effie's gay courage and imperturbable coolness I could not have done it, I am sure. One night we had to sleep at a little wayside station house on the way to Abbeville. The lines of communication there were of the first importance. Troop trains, munition trains, and food trains rolled up and down endlessly, and every vulnerable point was guarded by soldiers with fixed bayonets. As we approached the station house, I saw one of these sentinels approaching us, doubtless to inquire our business. We had been on the train since dawn, and had been dropped at a little siding. I stopped short as the *poilu* approached, feeling suddenly in the grip of fear.

Effie marched cheerfully on and was soon in animated conversation with what to me was an object of terror. They were both smiling and gesticulating, and when she came back, and I inquired what it was all about, she said : " Oh, he was telling me all about his wife and kids away back in Touraine." " One touch of nature makes the whole world kin." But there was not much sleep for me that night, on my hard pallet in the little station house, the boom of the guns, unceasing for one moment, was too near and terrifying.

We ended our marvellous pilgrimage at Etaples where we spent a week. Once a quaint old fishing village, familiar and beloved of artists, it had become one of the most stupendous bases of the war. The camps covered miles of the sand-dunes, hospitals, already full, had been built, canteens established—everything necessary for handling vast bodies of troops under all circumstances.

Effie said suddenly one day : " Mother, I'm stopping here."

I was not surprised. I had watched the way in which the whole new world was gripping her. I explained that we should have to go home first and interview Lady Bessborough, the head of the Bureau responsible for sending out women workers to the Y.M.C.A.

Effie was under the prescribed age, but her expert knowledge of French, and the fact that she was willing to take her car with her, disposed of all the objections.

In a week or two she crossed the Channel again, in full working kit, to remain there, except for short leaves, for the " duration." When the Armistice was signed, she went to Cologne with the Army of Occupation, and was absent from us for over four years.

CHAPTER FOURTEEN

THE WAR COMES HOME

THE Belgian refugees who had fled to our shores before the onslaught of the invading hosts, proved one of the problems pressing in the early days of the war. These unhappy people, many of whom had escaped with nothing more than what they stood up in, had to be welcomed, fed, clothed, and housed in some way. Our people rose to the occasion. Every city, town, and district offered hospitality, and most generously subscribed to provide what was expected to be very temporary accommodation.

Had any of us imagined how long that minor problem was to torment us, our hearts would have sunk into our boots.

I was appointed Chairman of the Hertford Committee, and never shall I forget going up to the Alexandra Palace at Wood Green, where hundreds were housed, waiting to be sorted out and sent to their various destinations. It was a spectacle calculated to move even a Stoic to tears, and to call up a feeling of passionate gratitude for having been born on an island, surrounded by the natural barrier of the sea. Although invasion of England or Scotland was then thought a possibility, if not a probability, one had the comforting feeling that it would be a risky business for the invaders, and that at least we should have warning sufficient to enable us to defend ourselves. The whole civilised world was still staggered by remembrance of the terrible goose-step march of the victorious German Army through the stricken streets of Brussels.

The majority of the refugees who flocked to our shores had escaped from the country districts, from the smaller towns and villages, many of which had been decimated and destroyed. Our party came from Roulers and had harrowing tales to tell of what happened there.

To see these poor people huddled in groups under the vast glass dome of the Alexandra Palace was to have a fresh and ineradicable conception of the infamy of war. They had not only lost all their worldly possessions, but many families were incomplete. One stricken father and mother, their heads bowed in unconquerable woe, had a story to tell of their daughter Yvonne, young and pretty, who had been unfortunate enough to attract the attention of the German High Command. They never expected to see her again.

Such tales were the daily bread of the invaded people, verifying the ruthless conclusion come to by Bernhardi in his book, *Germany and the Next War, i.e.* " Conquered peoples should be left with nothing but their eyes to weep with." Our refugees embodied this sentiment, carried into practice.

We had secured a fairly commodious empty house, which was hastily and adequately furnished by the gifts of the townspeople, and we were able to accommodate about a dozen people. They were a mixed crowd, and somewhat difficult to deal with, though intensely grateful for their safety and the welcome accorded to them. As time went on, and they grew sick to death of their protracted exile and the increasing stringency of living conditions, especially when food grew really scarce, we were driven nearly frantic. They grumbled a good deal latterly, and quarrelled incessantly among themselves. Quite often we had to settle disputes and try to pour oil on troubled waters. It was a ghastly situation for everybody, and one of the joys of the Armistice, for all concerned, was the restoration of the war refugees to their own country.

After all was over, my husband and I paid a visit to the war zone, and in the course of our journey called on some of our guests at their own homes. Their gratitude was most touching, rather overwhelming, in fact, and they vied with one another in showing us the most wonderful kindness and attention.

In the autumn of 1915, Zeppelin raids at regular intervals became a new menace to our peace in England. Hertford was rather unfortunately placed for these attacks, being in the direct route from London to the Essex coast, and also having in the vicinity two important factories—the Small Arms at Waltham Cross and Enfield—the location of which was of course well known to the German Intelligence Department.

We soon discovered from experience that the raiders had an ordered plan of approach and attack. They left their base and crossed the sea in mass formation, splitting up when they neared the coast, one-half converging on London by way of the Thames Valley, which, incidentally, enabled them to get a whack at Woolwich and other great munition centres. The other half came stealing through the Home Counties to attack from the north side. I don't think they were ever able to converge and unite successfully ; and their bombing of London, though bad enough in sections, could not be described as a magnificent or spectacular achievement in any sense. They were very persevering and industrious, however, for after they once started the raids, we suffered them right to the end. At first we were rather defenceless, but as time went on, our air squadrons became more than equal to all their tactics and onslaughts.

On October 13, 1915, the first big, concerted attack on London was made by the Zeppelins, and most dismally failed. We in Hertford, however, received the tail end of their cargo, to our undoubted distress and loss.

It had been a quiet and lovely autumn day. Effie had only arrived the night before on her first leave, and had, of course, much to tell us. Not as much as we wished to hear, for those young creatures were very reticent about their own experiences, and always made light and little of their work. Others, however, had a different tale to tell. The Zeppelin scare was in the air, and she said at dinner that night : " I'd love to see a Zeppelin raid. At our base there's no such luck."

Marvellous youth ! But she had her fill of bombing at her base and of sleeping in dug-outs before she was much older. Her father was out, paying his evening visits, and the house surgeon from the hospital had called with a message for him. Our evening tea had just been brought to the library, and the servants were at their supper downstairs, when suddenly we were startled by the most appalling noise, like an express train dashing across the sky. We had no warning sirens then, nor the comforting " All clear " signal when the danger was past, so we had not the faintest idea what had happened. We dashed out through the french window to the terrace, where it was absolutely pitch dark. But presently sinister lights began to glow. I find it difficult to describe just what happened in the three or four minutes the bombardment from the sky lasted.

The servants came dashing up from the kitchen, which was fortunate, as a few minutes later the ceiling crashed on their supper table. Had they been seated at it nothing could have saved them. We all, with one accord, rushed out by the french window to the terrace at the back of the house, too ignorant to realise the danger we ran, and merely curious to know what was happening. I find it difficult to describe that appalling five minutes' interlude, while the monster ship with its death-dealing cargo passed slowly over our town, visiting us last, and dropping eight bombs on our house and garden. The first of the bombs had destroyed the power station, so that the town was plunged in utter darkness. There were lights from the sky, however, as the incendiary bombs rapidly followed the explosive ones to complete the devilish work.

I had the feeling that it was the Day of Judgment, as we stood there, holding on to one another.

Presently the great monster sailed over us, so low down that it brushed the topmost branches of the old cedar tree on the lawn. The contact split the trunk from top to bottom, and later the tree had to be destroyed. In a few moments the roar of the powerful engines grew fainter and fainter, and finally died away. Then we re-entered the house, and by the aid of a pocket electric torch saw strange things.

We passed in by the french window, to find that all the hall furniture, some of it very heavy, seemed piled on the floor, and that there was no front door left. We could see right through into the street, where there was a good deal of noise and people moving about with torches and such-like. We managed to secure some candles from the sconces in the drawing-room, which appeared to have suffered least. The dining-room was stripped to

THE NORTH HOUSE, HERTFORD
BEFORE ZEPPELIN RAID

THE NORTH HOUSE, HERTFORD
AFTER ZEPPELIN RAID

lath and plaster, all the pictures on the floor—one large one on the top of the sideboard, which had lost a leg. The glass cupboard, which contained my small but priceless collection of Waterford glass, was face downwards on the floor, every piece smashed to atoms. Above the mantelpiece a small but rather darling little Chippendale glass still hung stoutly to its nail, and was not even cracked. Upstairs the destruction was even more complete. In my bedroom I was confronted by the spectacle of the seven-foot wardrobe lying on my bed, and in one wall, which had a little passage-way to the old wing of the house, there was only a vacuum, looking out to the stars.

The entire old wing, comprising five rooms, had collapsed, and some of the furniture was now in the front garden, hurled there by concussion which at the pressure commanded by the Zeppelins can work miracles.

Fortunately, no one was hurt, except Peter, the cat, who, sleeping peacefully under a bush in the front garden, had received the first impact and died at once. I must not forget to tell that one of our lovely Chows was found under one of the smaller beds, which had collapsed on her, when, I expect, she had run for shelter. She was not much hurt, but she showed signs of madness next day, and finally had to be destroyed. One of my hardest war tasks was to get her out of the kennel and lead her to the place of execution, as she would allow no one else to touch her. I believe that is the one thing I have never been able to forgive the raiders. I feel as badly, writing about it at this moment, as I did when that ghastly task had to be done.

While we were still poking about among the ruins, my husband came back, wheeling his bicycle, looking very white about the gills, some kind soul in the town having made haste to inform him that his house and everybody in it had been destroyed. When he found us safe, he didn't seem to think anything else mattered, and went off with his surgery bag to amputate the leg of a soldier, who was lying on the pavement outside the front gate and could not be moved.

About one o'clock in the morning, Effie and I went away to sleep at a friend's house, the Doctor making a shakedown in the comparatively safe drawing-room, though it had no window frame, and his improvised bed had to be sheltered by screens. As we walked up the street, holding on to the railings in the inky blackness, my hand touched something soft. The flashlight revealed our dining-room curtains, which apparently had been blown out of the house and twisted round the railings by some weird, invisible force. It may be guessed that we did not sleep very much that night.

Next morning the fun of the fair began. As I walked down the road, I saw it black with people in front of our house ; and that they were only prevented entering by the strong arm of the military and the police. Where they had come from at so early an hour Heaven knows, but there they were in hundreds, some having come long distances on bicycles, in motors, and horse vehicles, as well as on foot. Bad news travels incredibly fast, for there were no details at all in the morning papers. The utmost secrecy was observed right through, and all the public ever heard of the Hertford affair was " Air attack on London successfully driven off." Yet a number of people were killed in our town, and a great deal of property destroyed.

There were no press men or photographers, and I had to get military permission to have the photograph taken which appears in this book. I was determined to have it, and though everything connected with the bombing was carried off and sealed up, one half-burnt-out incendiary bomb was given to me as a memento. It is not a beautiful object. We used to think censorship and military supervision overdone in those early days, but no doubt all was necessary for the safety of the lieges and the discomfiture of the enemy.

That was the beginning of our long experience of war from the air. It lasted right on till the Armistice was signed. They only came on moonless nights, and I used to say the Man in the Moon got many blessings on the nights he shone on us. I never got used to them, and to this day the sudden, harsh note of a siren can make me jump. So the war came to Hertford.

We saw all the aerial battles over London, by which time our air force was sufficiently equipped to challenge the raiders. It was not a very thrilling or spectacular show. They looked like giant birds pecking at one another in the sky. Far more thrilling and appalling was the spectacle when an aircraft gun exploded into flames the cover of a vast Zeppelin, and its framework came hurtling to the ground at Potter's Bar. We could even see the poor charred bodies of the airmen falling from the sky.

We motored over to Potter's Bar next day to see the giant object, like a monstrous section of Meccano, stretched across the field. They were still removing bodies when we got there, and I thought of the German mothers, the Rachels who must weep for their children when the news came home.

They are buried in the churchyard, twenty or so of them, I believe, and I remember a great burst of indignation because a British mother had ventured to lay a spray of flowers on the grave.

I understood her action. These lads, like our own, were only doing their duty.

> " Theirs not to reason why,
> Theirs but to do and die."

They were in the grip of the great and merciless god of war, which spared neither age nor sex, and destroyed many lovely hopes in hearts for whom there could be no second spring.

CHAPTER FIFTEEN

THE MORNING AFTER

THE poor North House presented a pitiful spectacle in the garish morning light. It was in complete possession of the military, who were keeping at bay the crowd, anxious to get inside. A way was made for me, and when I stepped through the yawning chasm that had once been a dignified front door, I had a new and poignant realisation of what our Belgian guests had been through. And when, later, our model refugee, the gentle Madame Savarin, spat on the bomb I showed her, I could not reprove her. Eight bombs in all had been dropped on house and garden, and it was supposed that the spacious white frontage and the gleaming river behind had deluded the airmen into the belief that they were in the Lea valley, in close proximity to the Small Arms factories at Enfield and Waltham Cross.

I found my husband among the débris, looking rather stern and disturbed. He informed me that Effie and I were to go at once to Scotland, leaving him to make what arrangements he could. It was no use protesting, and as the authorities desired to seal up the whole place, pending examination for valuation and assessment of damage, we meekly acquiesced.

Trunks—not our own—were procured from somewhere, kind hands packed our clothes—and we got away. The kindness of our neighbours was indescribable. A common danger seemed to have united us all and broken down many barriers. By noon the sightseers, baulked of their desire to get inside, melted away, and the house was left to the owls and the bats, whom the Zeppelin had not been able to scare away from the great chestnut trees at the back, all ablaze with the glory of autumn.

We stayed at Kinghorn for five days, then heard from Jim that some neighbours, in a good house close by, who had nothing particular to keep them in Hertford, and having no desire to repeat the bombing experience, had decided to go for a spell to Bournemouth and offered us the house as long as we needed it. It was a timely offer, most gratefully accepted. Effie returned to her base in France, and to me was left the business of gathering up the fragments, previous to some scheme of reconstruction. It was some days before I summoned courage to go round to the house, which had been sealed up by Government orders Jim said very little, only went about his daily tasks with that queer, tight-lipped look, which might mean anything.

To this day I remember the awful feeling of desolation which swept over me when I came face to face with what had been my home. I had been proud of it. It was full of treasures which we had earned by the sweat of our brains, if not our hands. There were very few left. Glass and china had perished in the first impact. A cup here and there, with the handle off or a gash in its side, was all that was left of my Worcester and Lowestoft tea-sets. A Crown Derby dinner set, however, was miraculously saved. The night before the raid we had put up some of the officers marching through with a company to Colchester. A few friends had come in to meet them at dinner, and we had offered them our best. Had the dinner set been restored to its usual place, it would have gone with the rest, but it had been left in a downstairs cupboard, which the concussion had not reached.

I was only allowed to look, not to touch anything, until the Government Insurance Inspector came to examine and assess the damage. He provided, unexpectedly, the only humour of the situation. He was elderly, quiet, and polite, but not very sympathetic. It was just his job, with which sentiment must not be allowed to interfere. His line, of course, was to minimise the value. A table was set in the library, inventory sheets were spread, and we started in. While waiting for his advent, I had made an inventory too. Needless to say, it did not correspond with his, but had to be abandoned forthwith. The contents of the dining-room, where the worst destruction had been accomplished, came under discussion first.

He assessed the entire contents of the glass cupboard at ten pounds. I pointed out that some of the single pieces had cost that. He only shook his head and said that, in that case, every article should have been insured separately.

From that platform he never departed, and I quickly realised that, so far as even moderately adequate compensation was concerned, our cause was lost. A Worcester tea-service he assessed at twenty-four shillings. I soon gave up the ghost and left him to his job.

I got a meagre innings over Effie's clothes which, while she was living in uniform, had been hung in the wardrobe room, which the bombs had transferred in sections to the garden and the street. The old wing of the house collapsed entirely, and the contents of four or five rooms were now all mixed up with fallen masonry. The frocks had been rescued and laid out in melancholy array on a bed. It can be imagined what last year's frocks looked like, a torn mass of silk and lace and chiffon, stained with lime and water.

The sight seemed oddly to affect the valuator, though my shattered treasures had left him cold Perhaps he was a family man, and as he touched these garments pitifully could visualise the radiant youth they had once enfolded. He asked me what they had cost. Incapable of any accurate estimate, now that my sense of values had been shattered, I murmured : " Oh, about ten pounds."

He wrote down fifty pounds without a qualm, and hurried away from the sight as if he had had enough.

After the assessing was over, I was free to do as
I liked with the remains. I used to go round in the
early morning and stop till dark. Lots of people
wanted to help, but I was better without them.
My maid Florence, dear, faithful, incomparable
friend and helper, used to slip round now and again
to see what I was doing, then we'd just stand looking
round, thinking unutterable things.

Each day I missed something out of the little
store I had retrieved—a bit here and there, an old
salt-cellar or an odd cup and saucer. Speaking to
the policeman about it, he said he had several times
to turn well-dressed people out of the house, which
was open on two sides to the winds of heaven.
Souvenir-hunters, ghouls, eager to salve some
memento from the Zeppelined house. It was a
mean, unsisterly sort of theft, which I found it
difficult to forgive.

My storeroom, with its rich array of jams and
pickles and bottled fruits, freshly made at the
season's close, presented an appalling, sticky mess.
We were glad when the examination was finally
over, and the house could be shuttered up. Then
the question arose—what was to become of it, or
of us ?

There were immense legal and technical difficulties
in a situation for which no precedent or legislation
existed. We did not own, only leased, the property, so we did not know at first where our responsibility began or ended. It presently emerged that,
in some mysterious fashion, according to the terms

of our English lease, we were responsible for this damage and would have to rebuild for the proprietor at our own expense.

My husband naturally wanted to fight it out, to make a test case of it, in the law courts. But our old friend, Lord Craigmyle, advised us against it, telling us to pay up, no matter what it cost. His conclusion was : " The case simply bristles with litigious points, and I see it going on indefinitely and finally coming up before me in the House of Lords."

At the moment nothing more could be done, and as we couldn't go on living indefinitely in a furnished house, we communicated with the kind neighbour who had been such a friend in need, and found him willing to vacate entirely in our favour, and let us take over his lease, held from the Hatfield Estate. Cecil House was a very good house, roomy and well proportioned, and after we had made some alterations and improvements, suited us very well.

I had to carry them out myself, because one day my husband came down from town and said quietly : " I'm fed up with all this, so I've joined up, and have got a M.O.'s job with the 6th Black Watch."

He had been hammering at the doors of the War Office, I knew, for a good while, and must have told some fairy tales about his age. He was then nearly sixty. The next few weeks were hectic ; he had to arrange about somebody to carry on, get his kit

Dr. BURNETT SMITH
ATTACHED TO 6TH BLACK WATCH

together, and make ready for the next chapter in the upheaval.

One dreadful morning, in a " blast of Januar' wind," we said good-bye, and he fared forth to the fortunes of war.

Fortunately my hands were full to repletion. I had to get all the broken furniture out of the sealed-up North House ; arrange for our neighbour's stuff being removed, and once more reconstruct and establish a home.

Our household staff was sadly reduced. Several had gone to munitions—the young gardener had been called up—but we had still our faithful George Cook and Florence, buttresses sufficient for any tottering house. What I owed, and still owe, to the domestic helpers and friends I have had in my home, it is impossible for me to express in words. I say it now, lest by any mischance I should omit to say it later, which would leave a heavy debt undischarged. Those who have never known this devotion have missed something precious in life.

The garden at Cecil House provided the most difficult problem. There was a large space, fully an acre in extent, which had become during the last tenancy a builder's yard. There were concrete foundations to be broken up before even a seed could be sown or a root planted. There was, however, a good tree or two, indicating possibilities.

. I shall never forget George's face when I led him forth and explained that his job was now to make a garden out of what he saw in front of him.

Although good at shaking his head, he has a touch of the creative genius. Once having made his protest, he started in happily with pick and shovel. Bereft of the delectable garden so many had admired and envied, we were reduced, not even to a cabbage patch, but to a concrete back yard, suggestive of gun emplacements.

Before our tenancy of Cecil House expired, George had made the wilderness blossom like the rose. Its first crop had to be potatoes, in obedience to Government instructions, daily becoming more numerous and more stringent.

Altogether I had a very busy spring, no time to brood or lament, and the news from my dears on active service was good and cheering. I could see how the new life had gripped my husband, and how he was getting wrapped up in the " boys," finding in the care of other fathers' sons some assuagement of his own undying grief. I wrote as cheerfully as I could, for that was the first duty incumbent on the Home Front, not to depress those abroad with needless wailing and complaints. But some slightly discouraging facts had to be plainly stated because they admitted of no camouflage.

Through some mysterious finding of the law, which no lay mind can ever grasp, or hope to grasp, we were informed that we were liable to pay seven hundred pounds to the owner of the North House by way of compensation for the damage wrought by the Zeppelins. It had to be paid without delay, too.

We never then, nor at any other time, received a

penny of compensation for all we had ourselves lost by the raid.

These were the fortunes of war. We did not worry very much, nor make any loud complaint.

All one's sense of values was not only shaken, but completely changed. Things did not matter any more, only people. What was happening to them, and what was likely to be the end of this frightful struggle.

CHAPTER SIXTEEN

THE WAR—CONTINUED

THE winter of 1915–16 was one of the strangest in my life. Looking back on it now, I marvel that I was able to do so much, to keep my finger on the pulse of so many stirring, heart-moving things, and yet remain fairly efficient.

I had the entire responsibility of keeping our changed home together—of seeing that my husband's " substitute " (hateful word) even moderately attended to his practice, sit on endless committees, pour balm of Gilead on our troubled and tiresome Belgian guests, and latterly take an active part in the Food Administration in our own district. In addition, I dashed about to speak at camps and munition centres, and between whiles wrote hard to keep up my contracts. I never failed anybody, so far as I know, but it was I who had to foot the bill.

I had a lovely respite while my husband was with the 6th Black Watch at Norwich, preparatory to going abroad. He took a furnished house, and I went there with two maids, leaving the other to look after the substitute.

I found Norwich, one of the most beautiful of English cities, in possession of a Scotch invading host. The kilt was swinging everywhere, and it all seemed very dear and homely. Norwich people took the Highlanders to their hearts, and the kindness shown to officers and men alike was extraordinary.

I was naturally happy there, freed for the moment from overwork and strain. But I was deadly tired. Surely never in my life had I been so tired ! There were lots of alarms and excursions in Norwich, too. I never got used to being wakened in the night by the tramp of armed men, my husband being hastily called with the rest to " stand to."

The wind was often up in Norwich, and when quite sober, quiet matrons explained what they intended to do when the Huns should come marching up from the sea, there was no strength left in me. We had all our instructions regarding the route and method of our departure, when the dread moment came. The city fathers, mindful of the fate of Ypres and Louvain, had mysteriously spirited away the most precious of their priceless treasures, which were hidden in safety till the war was over.

We tasted a new form of menace while we were in Norwich, a bombardment of Lowestoft and Yarmouth from the sea. We were awakened about four in the morning by the rattling of windows and a dull boom. Familiar with the sound, I said to Jim : " That's naval guns, and they've come." He only laughed and told me to go to sleep. But when we got about we heard that a bombardment had actually taken place and much damage done. Rumour exaggerated, of course, though when we motored to the coast later in the day, we found the damage was serious enough.

Our old Hampstead friends, the Leightons, parents of Roland, of whom Vera Brittain has written so tenderly, were at Lowestoft then, full of pride over their gallant and beautiful boy getting ready to go out. I went to see them one day, and have a vivid memory of her, sitting up in bed, trying on a new hat, just arrived from Louise in Regent Street. I was awed when she told me the price was ten guineas. I had never in my life paid that amount for a hat, but as she said, " Why not ? " I might have done, had I been sure I should get ten guineas worth of satisfaction out of it. But I I am not Scotch for nothing. She was a brilliant, vivid creature, one of the best talkers I have ever met. She could illumine everything, and they were a devotedly attached couple, whom it was a pleasure to meet.

I greatly enjoyed my few weeks at Norwich, and it was a revelation to me to see my husband with the boys. They all adored him, and no doubt, in helping them he found some assuagement for his own irreparable loss. But I did not recover tone, as I expected, and when I ran over to Harrogate to spend a few days with a friend from Scotland, I was taken violently ill and had to have an operation for appendicitis. It was quite successful, and

I had a further spell of rest in a most comfortable nursing home. At the end of five weeks, in marched my lord and master one day, to inform me I was going home next day.

" I'm quite happy here, thank you," I replied " I'm preparing to stop here for the duration."

For nobody spoke of the war, kind friends brought me books and flowers. It was a lotus land. But I was taken home next day, according to plan. He was right, of course, as he generally was about all the things that mattered. It was no time for a restored and competent female to acquire the Nursing Home habit. Plenty of work was waiting at home, and after an interval I went out to France for the second time.

It was the same programme with a difference. The glow and glory was sadly dimmed, the spirit of the Crusaders only existing in patches. It was conscripted men I had to deal with now, and the material was less impressionable, full of doubts and questioning, talking of Fritz, not as an enemy, but a comrade in misfortune. There were gleams of glory, of undimmed and untarnishable heroism, of humour which illumined all the dark places, and made one unconquerably proud of the material that is the human race. But always the laughter was akin to tears.

One day, at Camiers, I was trying to make something of two hard-bitten old soldiers of the Indian Army, who had taken part in storming the heights at Dargai. They were middle-aged, hard-faced men, who had no illusions about war. It was just their job. They neither praised nor condemned it. After trying every device to get them to talk, I said casually : " It seems very quiet up the line just now." A more futile and banal remark could not well be imagined, but it struck a chord.

A slow glint came into one pair of eyes, and their owner said dryly : " Ay, but me an' Jock's gaun up on Monday."

They were of the brand that was more concerned about the punctual arrival of the rations, and who discussed their quality in scorching language. One could wish that the war profiteers could have over-heard some of the strictures passed by the men. They had a list of those who were to get Jeddart justice at the end of the war, if any survived to serve it out. " Plum and apple " was at the head of the list.

I was sent one day to a small forage camp at a God-forsaken spot, not far from the lines of com-munication, a kind of " No man's land " which nobody ever visited. Lectures and concert parties passed it by. It was too small and insignificant for it to be anybody's business. It was the kind of job I loved, and I rose cheerfully at four o'clock in the morning to catch the only available train. It was now almost unapproachable by train. And there were no cars to spare for the woman speaker. The distance in miles could not be far, but it took us till three in the afternoon to get there. We were frequently shunted into sidings to let troop, ammunition, and hospital trains go by, and there were no civilian passengers except myself in the train.

In course of time the train drew up at a small siding in the fields, and I was met by a sturdy little divinity student from Aberdeen, who was holding the fort there for the Y.M.C.A. When he went first to offer a bit of Christian comradeship, he had to sleep with a revolver under his pillow, aware that any night he might get his throat cut. His men were not soldiers, though they were in uniform, but rough east-enders, dock labourers, flotsam and jetsam of the streets, some of them with lawless, anarchic blood in their veins. They were the husbands of some of the women whose patient faces and un-fathomable eyes had often wrung my heart when I went to speak at Women's Meetings down east.

The fortunes of war had cut them off from the homely grime and glory of West Ham, and Canning Town, and Poplar, and those in authority were finding them a tough proposition. They had neither excitement nor thrill in that queer hiding-place, except perhaps an occasional airship hovering overhead. Their job was to guard thousands of tons of forage, required to feed the transport horses and mules.

We pottered about the camp till nightfall, then the men gathered in the tent to hear the message a woman had brought them from Blighty. I knew, when I was able to discern their faces through the tobacco smoke and the reek of the evil-smelling oil lamp, that I had my job cut out to interest them, and that only the grace of God would help me through. I got them after a bit. I knew all about the homes they had left, and I spoke straight from the shoulder, even venturing to touch on how hard some of them had made it for the women they had left behind.

When the talk was over, they crowded round to offer little bits of their personal experience. One particularly unattractive person, with a cast in his eye, inquired whether he could have a private word with me. We could only achieve it by going outside into the starlight, but I kept as near as possible to the lighted windows.

" 'Ere, Missus," he began, " does yer 'appen to know the Barkin' Road ? "

Did I know the Barking Road ? Yes, even some of its mean streets, where the tragedy and comedy of life are played out day by day.

" See 'ere, then, Lidy, thet was good talk, but it don't git fur enuff. Maybe I weren't all I should a' bin, back 'ome, but my missus, she ain't played the gime, she's played it low dahn on me, since I bin in this bloomin' war. I ain't 'ad no letter from 'er fur over four months, an' I carn't 'ear nuffin' abaht the kids neither. A bloke what lives dahn our street sent me word last week thet she's bin an' sold up the whole b—— shoot an' nobody knows wheer she is, an' the kids is in the Union. An' 'ere's me, stuck in this blarsted 'ole, an' nobody to hunt up them kids an' give *er* wot fur. Wot are yer goin' to do abaht it, Lidy ? "

It was a tough proposition, part of the irretrievable tragedy of the war in a nutshell. I did what I could, trying to comfort him, as I took down all the particulars in a book already bulging with behests, which I fancied would take me the rest of my natural life to carry out. I wrote hundreds of letters to relatives and friends of the soldiers in France, for my letters were not censored.

When I got back to England, I made the necessary inquiries, put the Salvation Army on the track, and found his story completely verified. His Missus was never found. She went down in the underworld. The psychology of the case was crystal clear. Tasting freedom of action for the first time, with more in her purse than ever before, she lost her sense of proportion. The separation allowances, which spelled untold riches in many poor homes, undoubtedly helped to intensify some of its tragic aftermath.

As I lay down on my queer little bed that night, thinking over these things, another side of this strange drama rose up, making me laugh in the darkness.

The day before I crossed the Channel, I was lunching at my Club in Dover Street, when I met an old friend, the wife of a London doctor, who had joined up for active service. She looked very smart; I had to rub my eyes, wondering whether I was making a mistake. However, she joined me at my table, and feeling very forlorn myself because my husband was away, I said something of a sym-

12

pathetic nature. She put her elbows on the table and laughed rather deliciously.

" Oh, don't imagine I'm lonely or disgruntled. I'm just having the time of my life. Nobody to grumble at me or say the meat's overdone, or ask where I've been or how much I've spent. In fact, *entre nous*, I've no more use for Dan."

It worked that way in a good many lives. I never heard what happened to that pair in the end, for Dan certainly came back, and they resumed their dual life—possibly with a difference.

All the war diaries published recently have much to say about the shortage of munitions and its effect on those engaged in the terrible and unequal struggle. I heard a good deal about it from both officers and men in France. Quite early in the war the men began to realise, or rather to fear, that they were not being adequately supported by those at home. Dealing with tired, harassed, and over-worked men, the officers had to keep from them facts which they knew only too well.

One officer put it like this to me :

" Business men in England are making fortunes out of the war in questionable ways. When I cannot get sufficient material to protect my own Battery, I am firing on German works made of concrete supplied to Germany by Britain through Holland."

That is a heavy indictment, and one fears it was not a solitary instance. How to apportion the blame for this monstrous crime is not easy. There is no chance now of it ever being brought home to the guilty parties. One can only hope that some-where, somehow, justice will reach those who, for filthy lucre, sold their fellow-countrymen to death.

I was very happy at Etaples with Effie and her pals. They were a gay and winsome company. Living on army rations, in restricted quarters, with very little comfort, they, too, seemed to be having the time of their lives. The reports on my child's war work warmed her mother's heart. From those in authority came the comforting assurance that it was absolutely tophole. One grateful and very experienced Leader said this : " Whenever we have a hard job or one we hesitate to ask anybody to take on, we go for Effie. No matter at what hour of the day or night the call comes, she is ready, tireless, resourceful, absolutely dependable."

If there was a cross, surely that testimony was Effie's crown.

A strange thing happened at Wimereux. In the hotel there I met a woman I had never seen before, who introduced herself to me.

She explained that she was there because her son, who had been at Rugby with mine, was seriously, they feared mortally, wounded in hospital. She was permitted to spend as much time as she wished by his bedside and was specially anxious to sit with him through the long night, fearing he might be lonely. To her surprise he did not seem anxious for her to do that, and after some discussion he said :

" You see, Mother, I'm never lonely in the night, for directly the lights are low Ned comes and stays by me till the dawn."

I make no comment on that, except to say that I believe it absolutely. Could anything be more in keeping with the great loving heart of the Father God and the living Christ than to send those safe with them in the Father's House to minister to their comrades in need ?

I had to hurry back for my husband's last leave before he sailed for the East. I am unable to describe that, it was too poignant.

I had often stood on the platform at Victoria or Charing Cross to bid a comrade good-bye, but this was different.

A little company of close friends had assembled to see him off—Lady Arrol, Maud, and their brother Ronald, who lost his leg at Loos. He was a boy to whom legs meant a good deal, but he went through his Calvary with a cheerful smile, saying he'd give his other leg, if it would do any good. In the face of a spirit like that, a woman who already had had her innings of life and love surely should have been dumb.

But when the troop train pulled out and the blackness of the tunnel swallowed all the bright faces framed by the brand-new pith helmets, I suddenly discovered that all the strength had gone from me, and that there was nothing left.

Unable to sleep that night, I had a vision of a great Judgment Seat, where kings and emperors, diplomats, politicians, wire-pullers, and profiteers will have to answer to the blood-stained hosts they ordered forth to fight and die ; a host reinforced by all the women whose hearts had been wrung and broken. It is a vision which some day, somewhere, surely will materialise.

CHAPTER SEVENTEEN

PROBLEMS FOR CIVILIANS

ABOUT this time the food problem became acute in England. It had been something of an anxiety from the start, as we cannot produce in our islands more than half what is required to feed our people. The freedom of the seas, therefore, is a matter of life and death to us. As the war conditions everywhere tightened, and the submarines became more and more active and successful, anxiety about Food became rather more than a problem. I spell it with a big F because so it loomed before the minds of all who had even a limited knowledge of what was going on behind the scenes. The ration card system, which some regarded as a joke, some as a nuisance, and the great majority as a totally unnecessary aggravation of the war, may be said to have failed in our country. The imploring official appeals and slogans : " Eat less bread "—" Save the wheat "—" Food will win the war "—left them cold. It was only when faced with actual shortage that they began to realise the seriousness of the position.

My work on the Food Administration afforded me

a lot of sidelights on the mentality of my neighbours and others with whom I came in contact. It is a very odd commentary on human nature, but it is certainly true that Food is a searching test of its quality. People will go cheerfully without new clothes or outside pleasure, or even fire, but touch their food, and there is instant revolt. We had quite a lot of surprising cases of food hoarding, as well as food wastage, some of them in places where one would have least expected it. My household was kept up to the mark by the faithful Florence, who deserved a medal for the way she weighed up the ounces and did all the things to conserve supplies which many people left undone. I became an expert, from whose lips calories and proteids and other heathen words flowed glibly, as to the manner born. The one I hated worst was " substitute." Quite frequently I said it should be expunged from our vocabulary, when we were through with the war.

I was not the only one it enraged. I met a woman in the street one day, who thus poured out the vials of her wrath.

" Please, I've tried to do what you said wiv them ' substitoots ' " (Oh, the scorn in her voice !), " but 'Arry, 'e won't look at 'em. Calls 'em messes, 'e does, wants 'is 'onest beef steak, an' I don't blime 'im, neither."

Another, to whom I had been expounding the virtues of bones, made into a good, nourishing meal for a family, cried indignantly :

" Feed me children on bones ! Good lor', 'as

it come to that ? No, thank you, Ma'am ; I'll get me mite o' meat an' bread an' butter as long as I can, an' when we carn't get them no more, well, I suppose we can starve."

What struck me so often was that they didn't believe in the economic urgency of the war and took the Government orders as a personal insult, to be evaded and defied whenever possible. They got educated towards the end, but it was a sorry job for those who had to help with the education.

There is no doubt whatever that bread *is* the staff of life, the staple food of the majority of households, and when it is threatened, it rouses frightful indignation—the sort that culminates in revolution. We were getting very short of wheat flour, and our English bread, made of Heaven knows what, was both unpalatable and indigestible. For some unexplained reason Scotland was never so hard hit as England by the food shortage. A friend in Dundee saved my life by sending me a weekly loaf of white bread, in which there was certainly no substitute for wheat flour. I received it gladly, for I was working frightfully hard and beginning to feel the strain. We were nearing the desperation line in the Food conservation business, when a new door suddenly opened, as it so often does in extremity.

The Central Food Administration discovered the value of the communal kitchen.

As Chairman of our Kitchen Committee, I went to London in company with another member, a delightful, practical, breezy person, to inspect the working of the big Experimental Kitchen in the Westminster Bridge Road.

It was a thoroughly interesting expedition for me and my colleague, and for the first time gleams of hope were dangled before our weary vision. The Communal or Central Kitchen is established for the purpose of supplying a large number of meals at the smallest cost. A first-class plant is necessary, the most up-to-date ovens, steamers, utensils of every kind. Also the cook must be an artist, as well as an expert, especially in war-time, when she has to disguise inferior ingredients sufficiently to make them acceptable to fretful, capricious appetites.

We found that the stores were purchased in bulk, so far as Government regulations would permit, that the cook and her helpers were highly-paid workers, but that the distribution of meals was undertaken by voluntary helpers, who each gave four hours' service per day. It was one of the most valuable bits of war service, given cheerfully by large numbers of women, who wore no uniforms and got very little recognition. Not that they were looking for it. They were glad to do their bit, to help to ease their own heartache.

No food was allowed to be consumed on the premises. The customers had to bring their own baskets or buckets to carry their portions away. The menu was hung in the window, and from it they made their choice. We went early, watched the food being cooked, imbibed some fresh information, then waited for the customers.

They interested me tremendously. It was a very poor neighbourhood, but it was not the visibly poor who came. Some quite well-dressed people arrived, pleased and satisfied with this new help for the problem of daily living.

A bank clerk's wife assured me it had been a god-send to her, as she was out at work all day, and they were both now assured of one good, nourishing meal.

A mother of seven told me, with tears in her eyes, that the kitchen had meant salvation to her family.

It all cheered and encouraged us, and I felt valiant enough to make another onslaught on the indignant mother who wouldn't demean herself to have any truck with bones.

We went back to Hertford and established our Communal Kitchen. It was viewed with supicions at first, as savouring too much of the soup kitchen or the penny dinner scheme. After a lot of explaining that there could be no suspicion of charity about it, and that we were merely trying to co-ordinate our forces and make our resources go as far as possible, the idea caught on.

The children were better fed, anyhow. Some of them through Zeppelin scares and other things were getting to look very peaky, and teachers told us they found it difficult to get them to concentrate on their lessons.

We suffered little respite from Zeppelin raids, and now we had acquired a regular system of procedure.

A Zeppelin night might mean anything in duration from seven or eight in the evening till four next morning.

As our system of defences was strengthened, the war in the air was continuous, until the monsters were driven across the sea again. A new form of aeroplane, called the Gotha, was evolved latterly; more daring, more destructive, much faster, and less vulnerable than the old Zeppelin. In addition to increasing scares, we had two attacks from them in Hertford, doing a good deal of damage to property, though no lives were lost.

The worst result of this perpetual raiding was the weakening of the morale of the civilian population. Of course that was its object. When the next war, of which some people write and speak with such cheerful confidence, comes, we shall not need to take all the precautions we then took. It will be all over shortly, and the people wiped out. There will be neither time nor opportunity for the weird nights, in the cellars, such as we had at Cecil House during the Zeppelin season, sheltering thirty or forty, giving them midnight tea, encouraging them to knit and talk.

But I went very little into the cellar. I preferred the open street, where I could listen and watch, knowing full well that the safety of cellars was largely imaginary, and that a bomb on active service, falling in the right place, would make short work of the cellar refugees. But it served its purpose, and we managed to live through those ghastly months. Looking back on them now, it seems like some fantastic dream.

The next milestone for me in these strange, travelling days was the sinking of the troopship *Transylvania* in the Mediterranean. It had my husband and his hospital unit on board. I received the news by way of Etaples, Jim having thought it wiser to wire to Effie first, in case of shock to me. There was, of course, no mention of the disaster in the newspapers. I had to wait several days for particulars, and finally he arrived home himself, looking like a picturesque and rather attractive bandit, in a blue Italian military cloak. He had lost all his kit and had not even a tunic to his name. The story, as he told it, was vivid and tragic.

It happened off the Italian coast, about ten miles from Genoa, at ten o'clock in the morning. The first torpedo damaged the ship, but not mortally. Had it been the only one she could have got away under her own steam. However, presently the second one came hurtling across the waves, got her clean amidships, and in a few minutes she sank. Five hundred men were drowned. Many more might have escaped had they had the courage to jump from the sinking ship, instead of waiting to be sucked down with her. My husband was in the water for some time, being picked up finally by a Japanese destroyer. It was a terrible experience, from which he never fully recovered. But after a brief leave, he got a new kit and was off again.

I had disquieting news from France too. Effie

was knocked down while standing beside her car, by a big, military French car, which did not even stop, nor its occupants make any attempt to pick her up. She miraculously escaped with a few bruises, and was able to send me a few lines from the Base Hospital, to which she was carried.

I applied for permission to go over to see her, but was refused. All the regulations were being tightened up about cross-Channel passages, only the relatives of the desperately wounded being granted permits.

Her temperature remained high for several days, and my anxiety was consuming. However, at last she was pronounced convalescent, so I had to cease worrying.

All sorts and conditions of people wrote to me about her from Etaples, explaining chiefly how absolutely indispensable she was to the Base. This, I expect, in case I might suggest that she should now come home for a spell. After three years' active service, she deserved it. But most certainly she did not desire it. Like Mr. Britling, she intended to see it through.

I expect my nerves were getting a bit ragged after all my active service, and I could not somehow take the same lively interest in what was going on. Nature, I suppose, was registering a protest that I'd better be taking stock of my resources.

Instead of it being the end of my war service, as I often rather dismally protested, it was but the prelude to the biggest bit of it.

I received an invitation to go to America on a mission for food, the shortage having become so desperate that the situation was serious. I had no hesitation in accepting. It was an honour I had never expected, nor sought after.

It came at the psychological moment, for I was physically and mentally exhausted, and in need of something to lift me clean out of the rut of depression into which I was gradually sinking.

All my family were on active service, and there was nothing to hinder.

I left England on January 7, 1918.

CHAPTER EIGHTEEN

AMERICA AT WAR

IT was not my first visit to America. I had crossed the Atlantic several times to visit my brother Alec, who was wheat-growing on the Canadian prairie. Being an excellent sailor, I was looking forward with a kind of wistful anticipation to the complete rest on the ship, where I would be free from Zeppelin raids, from Food problems, and from Belgian refugees. Oddly enough, I had forgotten all about the submarines! I went up to get the boat train, reflecting sadly that I had not a creature of my own to see me off.

The first surprise was to find that there was no boat train, only a few slip carriages attached and reserved on the ordinary train to convey the passengers to Liverpool. The name of the ship I did not even know, so great was the secrecy about everything observed by the authorities. We were sixty passengers in all, and the only other woman was Miss Bennett Burleigh, daughter of the famous war correspondent. She was going on a lecture tour, under whose auspices I can't remember. Our fellow-passengers were chiefly soldiers, Red Cross people, and government officials connected with munitions, food, and other war supplies.

It was a queer prospect, and never shall I forget the extraordinary picture presented by Liverpool Docks when, driven in a sort of Black Maria from the station, we beheld it in the fading light of that bleak winter afternoon. We had become familiar with the word camouflage, by which everything was supposed to be made to look like something else. The docks were full of ships which looked like nothing on earth, painted in strange hues in waving patterns, intended to blend with the waves and deceive eyes on the outlook for them.

Our vast cavern, one of the largest liners, capable of carrying about four thousand people, received the dismal sixty into its capacious bosom, where we were swallowed up. It was the very oddest experience. Everything seemed ghostly, shadowed, muted, even live creatures moving stealthily as if expecting some menace with which they must be ready to deal. The word " submarine " was not mentioned.

I was shown to my cabin, a millionaire suite, with a brass bedstead, a pink silk quilt, and a bathroom all to myself, accommodation that I knew existed, but which had never before been for the " likes o' me." There, with a queer sense of apprehension, I unpacked my clothes and waited for the engines to start up, so that we might swing out on the river's breast. Nothing doing. The stewardess arrived, cheerful, but not communicative. We dined at the usual time, a dinner such as I had not

seen for at least two years. The items which interested me most were white rolls and real butter,
which we had not had in our house for nearly a year.

I surveyed the company, and decided I was likely
to have a dull time. They were all middle-aged or
elderly men, some in uniform, all looking more or
less responsible, if not distinguished. How kind
they were to me ! How much I learned from them
during the next eleven days, I find it difficult to set
down. They were obviously interested in me and
my job, of which I was quite ready to talk. They
talked too, but very little about *their* jobs. The
secrets of the prison house which war had made
were in their keeping.

In our cubby-hole in Liverpool Docks, part of
the vast, grotesque camouflage, we lay for three
mortal days, eating, sleeping, walking about on the
deck, but not allowed even to step on shore or to
send a post card to any who might be interested.
It was no use asking questions, or throwing out hints.
Everybody seemed to have lost the power of speech
or comprehension. I did not worry very much, was
only excessively bored. However, I ate and slept,
and read and worked at the interminable knitting
without which no decent woman cared to be seen.
On the morning of the fourth day I awoke to find
that the scene had changed, and that in the silent
night watches the great ship had swung out on her
ghostly errand, and we were in strange waters off
the coast of Ireland.

After breakfast the Captain came down to my

13

cabin and gave some welcome explanation. It
appeared that the Germans had just launched a
new and powerful submarine, capable of staying
out for three weeks without coming to port for fuel
or victuals, and that she was reported waiting outside the bar to get us. I expect they had "All
clear" signals on the sea as well as in the sky.
Anyhow, there we were. His instructions were
slightly disquieting to one whose nerves were already
a little frayed by war's alarms. He told me I must
sleep in my clothes till further notice, examined my
fur-coat, and found fault with my shoes for not being
stout enough, advised me to wear two pairs of
stockings, and to put a few things handy in a little
bag so as to lose no time getting into the boat.

"About five minutes might be the margin, if they
get us, and it's well to be prepared."

I didn't get into a panic exactly, but I admit my
heart sank into my boots. I was below par in
health, and my courage was at a very low ebb for
the next few days, especially at the zero hours of
the long nights.

I found that our ship had become a sort of armed
cruiser, with guns at either end, manned both night
and day. Vigilant watch was kept, and we had
many scares, but I can't honestly say that I ever
saw the menacing hood of the periscope above the
troubled waters. The power and strength of the
new type of submarine meant that the danger zone
had been widened and extended. We were not
beyond it for about four days. We were all quite

cheerful, though when the short day closed, no lights were permitted in the open, and even to scratch a match or light a cigarette on deck was a major crime.

We had boat drill of a drastic kind every day. Even that had its comic side. One bright being had purchased at great expense a rubber suit, guaranteed to hold him up in complete safety in any waters. It had a sort of breastplate with compartments to hold chocolate, and brandy, and biscuits. The vision of this trusting soul bobbing up and down on mid-Atlantic billows, nibbling at his provender, was too much for us, and for him. After he had dressed up for our benefit, making himself look like one of the rubber toys the little ones play with in the bath, we never saw or heard of it again. Fortunately no emergency called for the testing of the rubber suit. One morning we were all happy to find that the life-boats had been swung in and made fast again—the guns covered up, and other signs, assured us that we were now outside the danger zone.

As we neared the other side, I began to feel anxious about my work. I had had a marvellous rest, which had restored me both physically and mentally, and was now ready for the next chapter of experience. The head of the American Red Cross, whose name I regret has slipped my memory, gave me some wise advice.

" I want to tell you," said he, " that the thing which will help you most in your work will be if you remember that we in America are not mere money grubbers and dollar hunters, but idealists.''

I am not fond of the word ideal, which has been prostituted to too many base uses, but I found his words recurring to my mind often during the next few pregnant weeks. It was not only wise but true counsel he gave, and when one faces and accepts the truth, the first round of the battle is won.

I have happy memories of that voyage, of all the good talk, the fun and laughter, the nonsense verses I wrote for the general amusement, but underlying all was the stern, deep resolve to see the thing through, so that the peace of the world might be secured for all time. Ah, me! Ah me! that so much self-denying effort should apparently have come to naught !

We sighted the Statue of Liberty in a flurry of soft snow, which, however, cleared so that we had a sunny ride up Fifth Avenue. I was surprised to find it swathed in flags, and imagined that there had been a victory while we were at sea. But it was only America's way of proclaiming that she was in the war. Proudly all the Allied flags waved together in the keen January wind. There was one I could not make out. It was white with red stars on it—the American war service flag, the stars representing the number of men who had left the factory, warehouse, or office to join the colours. In the windows of many private houses there was a little flag with one star, indicating that the only son had gone to the war. I soon developed a special heartache for the mothers whose boys were " over there." For no leave-boats crossed the Atlantic. For all it was a long good-bye ; for some good-bye for ever.

I was taken by fellow-passengers to the Plaza Hotel, which I saw at once was no place for a modest missioner, out to preach economy and conservation, even in a country where there was no shortage but which flowed with milk and honey, like the Promised Land. I changed my quarters next day, then waited for what might happen next. I was then confronted with the extreme meagreness of my credentials.

I had been told that my job was to tell the American people what we had done in the war, and particularly to impress upon them how urgently we needed the food they alone could supply. Six weeks' supply was all we had, and unless reinforcements arrived speedily, neither the soldiers in the field nor the civilians at home could be maintained. The only address given me was the British Bureau of Information on Fifth Avenue, which I naturally expected would issue their instructions and guidance. It was a fond delusion, destined to be speedily dispelled.

We certainly are, in some respects, the most casual people on God's earth, and if the outcome of the war had depended on our system of propaganda, then we should undoubtedly have lost it with great slaughter. I presented myself hopefully at the fine offices where the British Bureau was installed, for what purpose I have never discovered to this day ; unless as an address to which letters could be sent. It called itself a Bureau of Information, but apparently it had neither desire nor ability to inform anybody about anything. I was conducted to Mr. Geoffrey Butler, the Head of the department, and he received me very coldly, with a slightly bored air. When I inquired how I was to get to work, he replied calmly :

" Speakers are supposed to arrange their own meetings and find their own audiences. We have no machinery here."

A pretty steep proposition, I imagined, for a woman who knew nobody in New York. Across the border, in Canada, I had hosts of friends, but they did not need my mission, and I was accredited to the United States. The interview was of the briefest description, and as I was whirled in the elevator down to the street level, I asked myself what I was going to do next.

I was angry, of course, but even more perplexed than angry. What could it all mean ? Had I made some gigantic, unbelievable mistake and got across the ocean by some trick ? I felt just like a castaway on a desert island.

But the Scots grit in me came to my aid, and, like Robinson Crusoe, I faced the situation, called up all my resources and prepared for a fresh move. At first I was inclined to take the next boat home, and then vowed that nothing would induce me to do it.

After all, I was an accredited agent of the Government that had sent me out, and they were expecting me to do the job for which I had volunteered and been accepted.

But that was a pretty ghastly morning, and as I wandered up Fifth Avenue, and presently dropped into a Child's restaurant to have a chicken sandwich and a cup of coffee at the cost of a quarter, I felt like a down-and-out. Well, at least, I wouldn't spend Government money on riotous living. I never did. I ate a great many meals in Child's restaurants, where I found the study of human nature abundantly catered for. I once even met there a man who had never heard of the war! Also a German woman, who, though a naturalised American, was a devotee of the Kaiser, and informed me what New York would be like when HE came over to take up his new empire.

That afternoon a new door of hope suddenly opened. The late Dr. Jowett, then minister of what is known as the millionaires' church on Fifth Avenue, having seen my name in the newspapers, came to call on me at my hotel. I told him the whole story, which did not in the least surprise him. Other missioners had had the same experience. Shall I ever forget how kind, how comforting, how understanding he was? To me he represented the relief ship to the stranded mariner.

He said: " We'll get a meeting in my church, then you'll see everything will go well."

He knew that I could speak, for the last time we

met was when I went to speak at the annual meetings in Carr's Lane Chapel, Birmingham, of which
he was then minister.

He arranged the meeting in the hall of Fifth
Avenue Presbyterian Church, and the women
turned out in force. I had a great story to tell, and
knowing how much depended on it, I did my best
to tell it well. Its effect was electrical, and the
moment the meeting was over I was booked up for
drawing-room meetings for several weeks ahead.
It was very good to start the campaign among the
rich, for theirs was the power to get and to
give.

I had some marvellous experiences. The first
meeting was in the gorgeous mansion of Mrs. James
Speyer, and never shall I forget that audience,
their pearls alone would have financed any decent
war. They were easy to talk to, and most responsive. That day I met one who became one of
my dearest friends. Mrs. John Wallace Riddle,
whose husband was for some years Ambassador at
St. Petersburg. Her country place was at Farmington, Connecticut, where I spent some happy,
though necessarily brief, periods of rest.

She spent a large part of her fortune in building
and equipping Avon Old Farm, a secondary school
and boys' college modelled on the English public
school, plus every modern improvement. The
beautiful buildings, entirely the creation of her own
genius, are well worth a visit from any student of
architecture visiting the United States. She was

on board the *Lusitania* when it was torpedoed, and escaped by a miracle.

Out of the meeting at Mrs. Speyer's house arose many interesting events, among others a conference convened by chefs and cooks, presided over by Mrs. Speyer's butler, a silver-haired Scotsman, looking like an elder statesman. It was a wonderful audience to address, also a very important one, since in their hands rested much power to conserve food and prevent waste.

I owed to Dr. Jowett also a delightful visit to Princeton University, where I was allowed to speak to the students. The day I spent with the Principal and his wife stands out in happy memory.

I stayed about two weeks in New York, long enough to get my finger on the pulse and heart of America at war. Then I went to Washington to consult with that king of administrators, Herbert Hoover.

CHAPTER NINETEEN

I ARRIVED at the gorgeous marble palace which is Washington Station, about eight o'clock on a chilly morning, when there was snow on the ground and ice at the edges of the Potomac. I had made no arrangements for accommodation, forgetting the fact that, though the city was full of hotels, it was also full of a floating population, as well as inflated official staffs, all of whom had to be housed and fed. So once more there was no room in the inn. However, fortified by a good bath and breakfast, I left my baggage with the hotel porter and fared forth to seek one of the most powerful and respected men in America.

All over the lovely city, but chiefly in the vicinity of the Capitol and Government buildings, blocks of ugly wooden erections had sprung up, as they did in the London parks in war-time, so that administrative staffs never before even dreamed of could have somewhere to function.

Inquiring at the block devoted to the Food Administration, I was informed that Mr. Hoover could not be seen, as he was then in conference, which

would probably last all day. Nothing daunted, I
sent in my name.

He came out immediately. That was like him.
If something had to be done, the time to do it was
now. I did not need to offer any explanation. He
had heard of my work in New York. He said :

" I guess you've arrived right on time. I've got
two hundred food administrators from every State
in the Union next door. Come in right now and
tell them what you want."

Frankly, I was appalled. How could I face an
audience like that—not people requiring education
in the matter of food conserving, but experts every
one, up to the neck in the whole business. I think
I must have looked rather sickly, this shock following
hard on a night in the train. But the next minute
I was following my new Chief along the passage
to the Conference Room.

When we entered, it seemed to me very large and
full of men. At the desk a man was holding forth
about hogs in Chicago and their distribution, and
I sank into a chair to wait till he had finished. It
was some moments before I had courage to look at
the sea of faces in front. They were wonderful
faces, clean shaven, clean cut, with alert eyes and
a general air of complete assurance and efficiency,
which made me feel like a small, weak worm. I
remember taking off my hat, suddenly aware that
if I didn't, I must expire. There did not seem to be
a particle of air in the crowded, steam-heated room.

The hog gentleman sat down, and Mr. Hoover

simply announced that Mrs. Burnett Smith had arrived from England with something important to say to them : just that, and no more. If there was one thing in the world Mr. Hoover consistently conserved, it was words. Perhaps, had he been more prodigal of them, he would have been a happier President.

I got up, and, looking squarely at my audience, began to talk. They were the pick of America's business men, some of them great captains of industry, who had left their own affairs to answer the nation's call.

I had no plan of campaign, no prepared address. It is seldom I can speak from paper, even from notes. It is the audience which makes me sink or swim. I had a story to tell, of course, a poignant story of the Allies' need, for though America had come in, she had no actual realisation of what was going on in Europe. You cannot suffer much from a war three thousand miles away.

As I spoke, fear went from me and only the message remained. I knew it was getting home by the tenseness of the atmosphere. It is an extraordinary power, to be able to hold an audience in the hollow of one's hand, to be able to play upon it as on a harp of ten strings. No one knows whence it comes, but undoubtedly it is a power to be guarded against, otherwise it can be very dangerous. The demagogue who can thus move multitudes, unless he has other and greater qualities, can be a menace to the public weal.

I can only describe the effect of that morning's work as magical. When I closed with an appeal for the supplies of which we stood so desperately in need, they sprang as one man to their feet. There were tears in many eyes. They crowded round, and in a few minutes' time I was booked up to visit so many States that I saw myself stranded in America for the duration. That kind of emotional interlude would not be possible in England or in Scotland. I found the Americans in war-time an emotional people, strung up to the highest endeavour, capable and ready for any sacrifice. No great sacrifice, save the irremediable loss of so many gallant sons, was ever required of them. They were rich, powerful, and absolutely self-supporting. The freedom of the seas meant absolutely nothing to them.

That being so, their marvellous voluntary rationing was the more remarkable. It far exceeded ours. At home those with inside information had long been aware that our rationing was a bit of a farce, to be evaded whenever possible. We carried our ration cards about industriously, but most people got what they could behind the scenes. Again and again it was demonstrated that Food is the supreme test.

I had prepared the ground in New York, but Washington was the beginning of my long and strenuous Food and Propaganda Campaign from the Atlantic to the Pacific coast.

I stayed about a week in Washington, getting my

bearings and meeting a lot of interesting people. President Wilson was then at the White House, and I left my card with the soldier keeping guard with a fixed bayonet at the gate. I was surprised at that in the home of democracy, but it appeared that the President was very apprehensive of personal danger or attack. I did not meet him, though efforts were made on my behalf. He was never a very accessible President, I was told, and the war had sealed many of the usual avenues of approach.

I had a wonderful meeting in the Opera-House, attended by Lady Reading, wife of the British Ambassador, and a large number of notable people. I was removed from the hotel by the Under Secretary for Agriculture and his charming wife, and during my visit to them had many opportunities of meeting the most of the people who counted at that time. Besides the Hoovers, there were the Kellogs, the Daniells, the Franklin Roosevelts, Newton Baker, Secretary for War in the Wilson administration, and numerous others. I received many interesting and some surprising sidelights on American political and social life. Political, or rather, party feeling, ran high, and for outspoken criticism of one another they had us beat. It made the luncheon and dinner-parties most piquant.

There was fierce criticism of President Wilson by the Republicans—and I gathered that he was not a popular favourite on account of his aloofness and unapproachableness.

I was also deeply surprised to hear that the beloved Mr. Walter Page was not considered a very
successful Ambassador for his country. Hundred
per cent., even fifty per cent. Americans thought
him too pro-British. Some years later, when I
revisited Boston, I had some talk with the widowed
Mrs. Walter Page, and gathered from her that undoubtedly the war and all its hopeless entangle-
ments had broken his heart. Part of Hoover's
unpopularity in some sections was due to his par-
tiality for England. When I revisited Washington
later, on the eve of his Presidential campaign, and
told him how many of us in England were praying
for his success, he smiled a trifle sadly, I thought,
and said that would probably be against him.

I spent a good many odd hours at the Capitol,
watching senators and congressmen conducting the
business of the nation, and came to the conclusion
that, on the whole, England conducted hers with
more dignity.

It was all very pleasant, but they did not need my
message in Washington, and I was eager to get away.
At last Mr. Hoover, in the midst of his colossal
administrative work, whereby he bound all his
colleagues (including me) to him by hooks of steel,
found time to draw up what they call a " schedule "
for my journey.

He asked me whether I wished to stay in hotels
or " visit " in houses on my tour, and I replied :
" Houses every time, if they would have me." A
woman, travelling alone, learns nothing in hotels,

and has little opportunity for serious talk with anybody.

Already, even in enlightened Washington, I had sensed the need for some very plain speaking about the part Great Britain had played and was playing in the war. No doubt there was some gross misrepresentation and belittling, but there was also a good slice of just plain ignorance, which it gave me uncommon satisfaction to dissipate.

" They'll talk you to death in their houses," said the man of few words. I said I would risk it, and I was glad afterwards. Not only did I taste the warmth and glow of American hospitality, but I got to understand the mentality and the outlook of the people, and last, but not least, laid the foundations of several precious friendships which only death will sever.

From Washington I went to Boston, where I was entertained by Mrs. Nathaniel Thayer, one of America's foremost women in society and public service. She was Pauline Revere, granddaughter of Paul Revere, who took the famous ride with which Longfellow's poem has made us all familiar. She had all the beauty, charm, and high gifts of her ancestry, and was one of Hoover's right-hand helpers. She occupied rather a unique position in Boston, having her own office in the State House and a band of workers under her. She worked at her office every day for the full regulation hours, suffering no social claims to interfere. I look back on my visits to her with gratitude and deep affection, and we keep up a correspondence to this day.

Other dear Boston friends were Mr. and Mrs. Henry Lord, devoted supporters of the English-Speaking Union, Mrs. Barrett Wendell, and Mr. and Mrs. Templeman Coolidge, to all of whom I owe much of the joy of my American trip. Perhaps it is the old *Mayflower* tradition, or the Puritan strain in the blood, but most British people feel more at home in Boston than anywhere else in the United States.

Although I had a meeting every night and quite often one in the afternoon too, my mornings were free, and I explored Boston thoroughly, finding out all the ancient landmarks and associations, and quite frequently wishing American history books would be a little more accurate in their accounts of certain events in which the British were also involved. The literary traditions of Boston and Cambridge are engaging. Quite often, in my wanderings along Beacon Street, where he lived, and across the Common which he immortalised, I felt very near to the " Poet of the Breakfast Table," remembering how I had looked upon his benign face at Professor Flint's luncheon table in the far-back Edinburgh days.

A more delectable open space than Boston Common no city could possess. I spent many an hour there, and was often amused, recalling an incident my husband had related to me about his first visit. Interested in a monument or statue

14

which bore neither name nor date, he ventured to stop a well-dressed passer-by, and asked for information. All that was forthcoming was this : " Say, stranger, I can't tell you. I've been coming along this block every day for five years, and I never saw that statoo before."

There were some pleasant half-hours, too, at the Houghton Mifflin Publishing House, discussing literary matters with Mr. Ellery Sidgwick, the Editor of the *Atlantic Monthly*. I was proud when he gave me some pages of space in the magazine, which enabled my message to reach many with whom I could never otherwise have got in touch.

Christian Science is one of the most powerful forces in American life. The gorgeous Mother Church in Boston, a monument to Mrs. Baker Eddy's personality and teaching, was shown to me by the Editor of the *Christian Science Monitor*, one of the ablest and sanest of American newspapers. It was an enormous relief to me, even to handle it, after the smashing headlines and general hysteria of much of the daily Press. Its articles were always well informed and authentic, and, generally speaking, ahead of time. The English Editor informed me that, money being no object, he could tap the most exclusive and authentic sources of news. No expenditure in that direction was ever called in question.

I have never quite understood the tremendous and growing hold of Christian Science on people everywhere. I found in the States that faith-healing was a powerful adjunct to its other doctrines, and that all the devotees of Christian Science seemed to have achieved a calmness of mind and spirit which was of service to them in living. On the ship coming across, a prominent Christian Scientist, who was sometimes brought to book for disobeying the regulations about lights, etc., in the war zone, assured me light-heartedly that nothing would happen to the ship while he was on it. It seemed a comforting assurance which, however, the rest of us did not share. The only active devotee I had known in England was Lady Astor. She came into my room one night in a house in Glasgow, where we both happened to be guests, and expounded her belief in the most engaging way, being desirous of easing the heartache from which I was at the moment suffering. But though I didn't grasp it then, nor have I since, the fact remains that it comforts and steadies thousands of perplexed hearts and gives them some anchorage.

I closed my visit to Boston that time with a great meeting in the Opera-House, one of the most moving, I think, of the whole series.

In the vestibule great was my amazement and delight to be greeted by a Scotch parlourmaid, who had been years with us at Hampstead, Nellie Malcolm, who had emigrated and married in the States. It was a bit of home for us both, and we watered it with our tears.

Letter from Mr. Henry B. Endicott, Food Adminis-trator for the Commonwealth of Massachusetts.

STATE HOUSE, BOSTON,
April 15, 1918.

DEAR MRS. BURNETT SMITH,—I wish I could make you know how much real good to Boston your coming here has meant.

It so happens that in the last seven or eight months I have had over a hundred labour strikes brought to me to arbitrate and to mediate, and if I had had you with me at many of these sessions, my job would have been lightened.

I have never heard any man or woman paint, in words, so clear a picture or bring the war home so quickly and clearly as you do. After listening to you, everything else seems petty and small. We have a splendid people here in the United States, but we are 3000 miles from the actual war, and it is hard for us to understand the real responsibility which rests upon us.

Words like yours have a tremendous effect at this time.

Mrs. Thayer tells me that you may come back to Massachusetts for a rest. I am going to urge you to do this, by all means, if possible. Don't fear that we shall urge you to make even one speech here, unless you desire to make it. We shall want to rest one who has rendered our city so signal a service, and my home will be always open to you.   You may be sure that Washington will be fully informed as to the great good you have done here, simplifying all our tasks.

With very best wishes.—Yours very truly,

HENRY B. ENDICOTT.

CHAPTER TWENTY

THE MIDDLE WEST

FROM Boston I journeyed to Pittsburgh, visiting several little towns *en route*, and speaking in every one.

Howard Heinz (of fifty-seven varieties fame) was Food Administrator for the State of Pennsylvania, and wielded great influence by reason of his high character and organising powers. The Heinz business, originated by his father, is one of the romances of American industry, and a monument to his genius.

I spoke to hundreds of their workpeople at the great factories, and saw most of the processes whereby the people's food are handled. It was a revelation in perfection. A great fortune has been built up, of course, because there never is any slump in food consumption, except when the money is lacking to purchase it. Never was wealth more wisely used and distributed, and Howard Heinz is one of the best men I have ever known ; he is absolutely tireless in well-doing. The ideals of which the Director of American Red Cross spoke to me on the ship are carried out in his life. I asked him one day why he was not permanently in Washington helping to guide and shape his country's destiny. He replied that the atmosphere was uncongenial to his temperament, and I understood something at least of what underlay his words. But just so long as men of goodwill and high endeavour stand aloof from public life, there is less hope that it will reach or maintain a high standard. But he did tremendous work in the war, and was one of Hoover's most efficient and trusted allies.

Pennsylvania, the Black Country of the United States, interested me enormously. All along the lovely valley of the Alleghany River were dotted little townships, outcome of the mining and great steel industries. All sorts and conditions of people are there, from all ends of the earth. The cosmopolitan nature of American citizenship and its attendant problems were brought home to me again and again in that teeming district. One night, in a queer little meeting in a queer little town, I was told there were fifteen nationalities represented, all of them living their own lives, eating their own national food, and speaking their own language. Thus is American government complicated by the alien strands among its people, but the next generation will be different. Born and reared in the land of their parents' adoption, they will hold less passionately to the " old countries," which, most probably, they will never see, though the dream of their fathers and mothers was to earn enough in the Land of Promise to take them home again to spend the evening of their days and sleep with their kindred dust.

Pittsburgh interested me rather specially because of its association with my fellow-countryman, Andrew Carnegie. His benefactions, in the shape of noble and well-endowed buildings and institutions, are a memorial to his lifework. I admired them, of course, but it was far more comforting to me to find his name held in such deep respect. I had heard rumours in Scotland of his hard treatment of his employees, but could not find the smallest confirmation, though I asked a great many questions in quarters where there would have been no hesitation in blurting out the truth, however unpalatable it might be.

It was very pleasant among so many kind friends, and there was plenty to do in that tremendous hive of industry, but I had heard that the Middle West was sadly in need of active propaganda, owing to the strength of the German element and its anti-war, or rather anti-British sentiment. I departed to my task prepared for difficulties, but not for the active hostility I had to face. I was to prove that love of country is one of the deepest and most enthralling passions by which the human soul can be influenced and swayed. It burned like a white flame in mine, when I found how Britain was misrepresented, belittled, and shamefully lied about. We, of course, had practically attempted very little propaganda while the war was in progress, our minds and hearts and hands being full enough of other matters, so the detractors had it all their own way.

I will describe one of my experiences in the Middle West, which may possibly prove the point I wish to make.

I arrived one afternoon at a little township in Ohio, where I was scheduled to speak the same night. Everything connected with my speaking campaign was arranged from Washington through the various Food Administrators in the districts. Sometimes the negotiations fell through, and there was some confusion about the meetings. But at this place there was no accident, nor even careless-ness, but a deliberate attempt to prevent the " Englishwoman," as they called me, from deliver-ing her message. My name was beginning to be known, for I had all the newspaper publicity I wanted, sometimes more. Quite frequently enormous headlines announced the fact that the " Zeppelin lady " had arrived.

There was no one to meet me at the station, but I got into a ramshackle old " auto " and was rattled down to the only hotel in the place, a typical one in such little towns, bare and uninviting, with a bar in the hall and a wide window, with some lounge lizards, hats over their eyes, dozing in their rocking-chairs. It was, however, amply furnished with spittoons. I had noticed the signs above the shops in the Main Street—German, every one ! When I inquired of the man in shirt sleeves behind the counter whether I could have a room, he said :

" No, Mam." Just that and no more. I then asked for the Food Administrator by name, but he shook his head, evidently knowing nothing about him. I did not know what to do then. The only train had gone and there would not be another till next day.

I asked very politely whether I might have a meal, and that was not refused. While I was consuming it with a very doubtful appetite, the Food Controller arrived, in an obviously agitated state. He was full of apologies, but, faced with some straight questions, admitted that there was no chance of a meeting, partly because nobody wanted it, and partly because the Opera-House, the only available hall in the place, was booked for some sort of a children's demonstration that night.

" Well, what's to be done ? " I asked. " I'm here, and I can't get away. Also, that engaging gentleman behind the counter says I can't have accommodation."

" Oh, I'll see to that," he replied, and left me to ruminate on this discouraging situation. He was some time gone, and when he returned, obviously the sky had brightened.

He had secured the room, and also confided to me that there might be a chance of my being allowed to say a few words by way of an interlude at the evening's entertainment. I didn't mind either way. I have no recollection of being disturbed or upset by such episodes. Courage will come if one has faith, and mine never faltered.

I lay down on my bed and had a good sleep, for

I was beginning to feel the strain of so many nights in the train. How the American people survive their mode of night travelling, I can't think, but they do.

At the appointed hour my friend came to fetch me to the Opera-House, explaining as we walked towards it how difficult everything was, and that though the Mayor would be in the chair he hadn't an idea whether I, though the accredited emissary of two Governments, would really be allowed to speak ! What a blessing is one's sense of humour ! My ineradicable flair for seeing the queer side of things has gotten me out of many a tight place, and I felt sure would get me out of this one.

We arrived. I was given an obscure seat on the platform, from which I could survey the audience, which packed the place. There were lots of children in gala dress, for whom a concert had been arranged, but about half the audience were grown-ups—very typically German grown-ups—and their faces were not particularly attractive.

There was an interval in the middle of the affair, when the Mayor got up, very red in the face, explaining about the woman on the platform and begging for her a quiet hearing. With laughter in my heart, if not on my lips, I approached the front of the platform and stood before the footlights. My objective was a serried row of highly upholstered German matrons in front. I had been studying them for some time, and decided they were the front line.

I began my story very quietly and gently. It required some finesse to tell about happenings in the war zone on both sides of the English Channel, since some, if not all, were an arraignment of German war tactics. Part of such success as I have achieved in public work and speech is due to the fact that I have never attacked anybody. In all the American campaign I never once mentioned the Kaiser's name, nor called Heaven to witness the guilt of the German war lords. I dealt with war in the abstract, as a menace and a curse to the peoples of all countries. It was a sound scheme, which produced the desired results and left no enmity nor bitterness behind. My line that night was pathos. I had registered a vow that I would make these Teuton matrons shed some tears for the woes of the world, or perish in the attempt. Incredible as it may seem, I succeeded. They received me in silence when I rose, but when I sat down the applause was rapturous. When the thing was all over, the German matrons conducted me, like a bodyguard, to the hotel, where they had what they called " a nice visit with me," asking all sorts of questions, about my home, my husband, my children, where I got my clothes, and what they cost.

It was a triumphant end to a truly awful evening. Next morning, all smiles, the distracted Mayor arrived with congratulations, assuring me that it was impossible to calculate the good that had been done.

The hostile landlord—Mr. Adolf Shultz—smiling too, declined to take any money for my entertainment.

.   .   .   .

I suffered many things from chairmen at some of these queer meetings.

One night a flamboyant gentleman, in the course of his introductory remarks, said that I had lost three sons in the war, and was, therefore, entitled to a sympathetic hearing.

I had to think rapidly as to what course I should pursue when I got up. I had no sons at all in the war, only a husband and a daughter. Should I, at the outset, explain this or leave it alone? To deny the Chairman's statement would be to embarrass him, quite as much as he had embarrassed me. I decided to ignore him altogether. When the meeting was over I inquired from what source he had obtained all these erroneous personal details. He smiled airily. All he said was :

" After all, the thing is to get the right atmosphere, isn't it ? "

I don't understand that mentality. I give it up.

Though I had some hard times in the Middle West, where the best of the wheat comes from, and where the people have tremendous vitality, I had also some very wonderful days in Cleveland, in Chicago, and with some delightful relatives in St. Paul's, Minnesota. While there I stole two days from my schedule and went by night train to Winnipeg to meet my brother, who came east from Brandon. That was a precious interlude, which helped me through a good deal. I could see that he was a little puzzled to understand just why I should have undertaken such a tremendous job, or what good it was likely to do.

I didn't try to argue or explain. His attitude was one more proof of how difficult, if not impossible, it is to realise a war three thousand miles away.

CHAPTER TWENTY-ONE

INTERLUDES

THE Women's Clubs naturally made many requisitions on my services. That was to be expected. A really efficient Women's Club on active service in the United States leaves nothing to chance. Every opportunity for information, or fresh light upon any subject under heaven, is seized with avidity.

The Club life, supplemented by complete organisation for war, was a vast, unfathomable sea in which I was quite frequently engulfed. American womanhood, organised for war, was indeed a remarkable spectacle ; it was over-organised everywhere, and in consequence there was some overlapping and wastage of effort.

American women take their Club life far more seriously than we do. The majority of Club members in England and Scotland regard their Clubs as occasional rest-houses and rendezvous, and except in special instances do not mix them up much with social or political activities. I was a member for several years of the Old Lyceum, which came nearest to the American conception of what Club life should be.

One of the main objectives of the Women's Clubs in the States is uplift, and they make frantic endeavours to achieve it. Now uplift is a very curious word, capable of many interpretations. Totally devoid of any ambition to uplift anybody, or to be uplifted myself, it was sometimes difficult to fit into the atmosphere. They were all so intense, so talkative, so insistent on the uplift, that I faded out mentally, feeling that my plain tale from the hills, or the sea, rather, was hardly in tune with their high aspirations and endeavours. I did my best, but was always more exhausted by a Club afternoon than by the largest meeting in a public hall. It was the personal pressure brought to bear, the desire to squeeze out every ounce or atom one had to give which left me limp. Even the fun which I got in totally unexpected quarters, and " unbeknownst " to the earnest souls who unwittingly contributed it, hardly relieved the exhaustion of these terrific afternoons.

I liked best the little Clubs in the villages and very small towns, where there was only a handful of women, and it was easy to see what an important part their Club played in their lives. I was at home among the working women, the wives of the farmers and the tradesmen, and owed them many happy and profitable hours. They were quite absurdly grateful for the small service I rendered so willingly, answering all their questions, trying to tell them what life was like in war-time for their sisters across the seas.

I was greatly impressed by the capacity of the ordinary American housewife to widen and project her interests far beyond the confines of her home. It made her at once a better housewife and a more intelligent companion. The completeness of the heating and labour-saving devices in quite simple houses frees the housewife from much drudgery, and, in consequence, she has more time to devote to what she considers higher things. I am not sure about their always being higher. My estimation of housekeeping has always been that it is one of the most exact and important sciences in the world, of vast moment to the individual happiness and the national weal. When I hear a woman say lightly : "Anybody can keep a house, and anyway, an hour or so in the morning is all it need take of a woman's time," I chalk her up either as a shirker, or an incompetent housewife. Homes are not built up that way, not the permanent sort, which are the shield and buckler to those lucky enough to find shelter under their roofs.

My home has always taken precedence of my work, and when anything had to go by the board, it was not my home. It was an attitude of mind incomprehensible to some of my American friends, and I could see they didn't believe me, anyway.

I could not help observing that the Club absorbed too large a share of time and attention on the part of many women. I am unable to say what effect

15

this had on home life, though I had some qualms about it.

I had the privilege of seeing so much beautiful home life that I hesitate to record the impression that it seemed in some odd way more detached than ours. Husbands and wives seemed to go their own separate ways a good deal more than is usual in our country. There was decidedly less comrade-ship. As this may have been only a fleeting impression left on the mind of a bird of passage, to say more would be at once an impertinence and an intrusion. Especially as, from the highest to the lowest, they opened their doors to me and made me welcome to all they had.

Before I left New York, I spent a couple of nights at the Rockefeller place on the Hudson by the invitation of Mrs. John D. Rockefeller, junior. On that estate the different members of the family have their own houses, but they are all within hail of one another. It seemed a delightful, patriarchal sort of existence.

The life in that beautiful but rather austere house was very simple. Hers was one of the few American homes where there was a considerable family. As they gathered round the table they were a lovely sight. She was not only kind to me, she had kind thoughts for people she had never seen. Happening to comment on the deliciousness of the plum cake at her tea-table, I said I wished I could send my slice to my husband, who was very fond of it and had not tasted any for four years.

Unknown to me, she had her *chef* bake a large plum cake, and in some mysterious fashion got it conveyed to England and delivered at my house. I found it there when I got back. This kind deed was on a par with many others, which I can scarcely recall now without tears. I have received it in all kinds of homes : the simple farmhouse, where I felt so specially at home, and where I would be allowed to pare the potatoes or mix the salad ; the shack by the wayside where the " Boss " would cut and bring in the logs from the wood-shed, and where there was good talk by the fireside to the pleasant music of bacon sizzling in the frying-pan. The houses might differ, but the hospitality was the same, effortless, kind, and never failing—without money and without price. We have much to learn from American hospitality. Ours suffers by comparison.

Owing to the stringency and the narrow limits of my " schedule " I had not as much opportunity as I desired of seeing something of the educational and college life. Except for a visit to Princeton and a meeting at Columbia, I did not come in contact with students, nor even see the insides of the splendid women's colleges, which are so outstanding a feature of the American educational system. Nor had I much opportunity of meeting those of my own craft. I was anxious to get in touch again with Gertrude Atherton, but she was in the Far West when I was in the Eastern states, and *vice versa*. One spare evening I was invited to meet a little coterie of women journalists.

It intrigued me very much to hear them so frankly discussing their work, their chances, and their " scoops." It was all suggestive of a more complete comradeship than we have at home, fewer jealousies, probably because the market is less crowded and competition in consequence not so keen. There is, or was then, more room and opportunity for all. The women did not seem to enjoy shutting themselves up in watertight compartments, but were happier working together. I have memories of tremendous luncheon parties organised by the war women, with hundreds at the guest tables, and much talk of varying quality and unmeasurable quantity. At one Miss Ann Pierpoint Morgan took the chair, while Commander Evangeline Booth and I were the principal speakers. I carried away an impression of hectic unresting activity of mind and body. I often wondered how they stood the pace. Possibly it was as well their spell of war enthusiasm was shorter than ours, else a considerable proportion must have succumbed.

．　　　．　　　．　　　．　　　．

Through the kindness of his sister, Mrs. Cowles, wife of Admiral Cowles, whom I met with Mrs. Riddle at Farmington, I had an interview in New York with Ex-President Theodore Roosevelt. An impression of extraordinary driving force remains. One could see how he was chafing at being denied opportunity to take active part on the fighting fronts, where undoubtedly his gallant spirit would have been at home. He asked me a great many

questions, some of which naturally I could not
answer, about our equipment, the disposition of the
troops on the different fronts, and in what degree
the temper and morale of our civilian population
were standing the strain. There was quite a small
crowd waiting to see him in the anteroom, indicating
the power of his personality.

I met a number in America who deplored that
Roosevelt had not been allowed to take a hand in
the game, even some who thought he might have
proved a deciding factor. Probably he was better
left on the safe side of the Atlantic. In certain
world crises such red-hot enthusiasm is sometimes
needed, but when it begins to function, some
perilous and even disastrous moments are likely to
ensue. He reminded me in some ways of our own
Winston Churchill, and brought back to my mind
one night when I happened to sit next him at dinner
in London. There was the same nervous play of
virile, restless hands—I recall him now as one who
seemed to be consumed by an inward fire.

．　　　．　　　　　．　　　．　　　．

A few more small cameos stand out in the back-
ground of memory.

At a luncheon given for me at Dayton, Ohio,
home of the National Cash Register—I sat next to
Wilbur Wright, who, with his brother Orville, was
the inventor of the first flying machine in the United
States. Like most creators, he was a modest,
retiring person, who did not in the least wish to
talk about his achievement. I did, however, hear

a little about the experiments in the workshop and
on the waste lands, and found that his faith in the
future of flying was fixed and unassailable. He
believed that man was made to conquer the air as
well as land and sea. He must now be watching
with intense interest and growing satisfaction the
units and squadrons scouring the skies, adding
triumph to triumph, linking up the remotest ends
of the earth. I can't imagine him troubling himself
about the fresh problems this proximity is creating
every day. Science having annihilated distance,
must shortly apply itself to the task of instructing
men how to live together in unity, else how is
civilisation to be preserved ?

Another day I met in the train, going to the
Naval Base at New London, a bunch of blue-uni-
formed navy lads, with their jaunty little caps set
at a perilous angle on their bright heads. My
heart warmed to them, and after watching their
antics for some time, I summoned up courage to
speak to them. Walking up the corridor, I said
pleasantly : " Would you boys like to hear something about the British Navy ? I come from
England, and could perhaps tell you some things
you might like to know." They looked slightly
taken aback, but soon gathered round, some squat-
ting on the floor and on the arms of the seats. That
was a good hour for me, and for them, for though
I could not answer all the technical questions they
showered on me, I could give them a good deal of
first-hand information about what our Navy was

doing in the war. It was one of the best bits of propaganda I had a chance of doing.

A great night was at Philadelphia, after the Armistice was signed, and they were celebrating what they called British Empire Day. Summoned by special messenger, I proceeded to Philadelphia, only arriving at the Opera-House after the proceedings had begun.

It was a gay and brilliant spectacle, every unit in the vast assemblage roused to the highest pitch of enthusiasm because the hideous cloud of war had lifted, and people *could* be gay and light-hearted once more. The flags of all nations almost smothered the place, and the platform presented a pageant of colour, too, with resplendent uniforms, sparkling medals, and happy faces.

There was a complete orgy of talk, speech after speech from the soldiers of the Allies, all relating and extolling the deeds of valour performed by the countries and the regiments they represented. How they had managed to get such a galaxy of stars together I can't imagine, for the " peace " was not yet a month old. As every country and every regiment presented its glowing tribute, and nothing had been said about Scotland, I began to be very uneasy. Turning to a rather glum-looking officer by my side, encouraged no doubt by the strip of tartan on the cap he held on his knee, I said :

" Where do you come from ? "

In good broad Scots he answered : " I come from Paisley."

" Well, aren't you going to get up and say something for Paisley ? "

"No fear," he answered, with a grim look on his face.

My heart by this time was full to bursting about the part my little country, land of the mountain and the flood, had played in the war, so that I could hardly bear myself. I thought of the decimated Scots regiments, of the villages where there were mourning women in every house, of the glens from which youth had been entirely wiped out, leaving none but grey-beards and babes in arms, of the gallant 51st Division to which my husband was attached, and when my turn came to speak I had only one thought in my mind.

It was at the very end of the programme, and I had a great welcome, partly, perhaps, because I was the only woman speaker, and partly because I was no stranger in Philadelphia and had many Scots friends in the audience. I could not, at this distance, give any résumé of my speech. I can only remember the beginning, which was something like this :

" We have had a wonderful evening, and among so many thrilling records of deathless heroism it would be invidious to draw any distinction. Only one tribute has not been paid, and I am glad to have crossed the seas and arrived in time to tell you that it was Scotland won the war."

It was a wild, extravagant challenge, but the house rose to it. The din was indescribable. The cheering could not be stilled.

Then I had to justify my contention, and I did my best, weaving for them a web of fun and pathos, of glory and the laughter that is akin to tears.

There was an anticlimax at the end.

When I sat down, a resplendent being in the blue-and-silver French dress uniform dashed forward and knelt to kiss my hand. The " Auld Alliance " between France and Scotland come to life again ! I was so embarrassed, I rushed off the platform and did not sleep a wink that night.

Next morning the two-inch newspaper headlines took away my breakfast appetite.

" Scotswoman says Scotland won the war."

I hoped that little interlude would be buried, as it deserved, in oblivion.

But it was a vain hope. At a London reception some months later, a woman I had never seen before dashed up to me and said :

" Remember Philadelphia ! "

CHAPTER TWENTY-TWO

DOWN SOUTH

WHEN I returned from the Far West, Mr. Hoover asked me if I would go down South to talk to the negroes about Food conservation. I thought it an odd question at the time, as surely my job was to go wherever I was needed, and could be of the most use. I welcomed the opportunity to see the South, with which is incorporated some of the most vital and moving pages of American history. The very words " North and South " call up poignant memories of the Civil War for the freedom of the slave, one of the most epoch-making struggles in the epic of the human race.

It appeared that, though not heavy drinkers, the negroes are gross feeders, and simply paid no attention whatever to advices and recommendations from Washington as to the strict conservation, amounting in some cases to elimination, of certain articles from their bill of fare.

I went first to North Carolina, where I was entertained at a flourishing little city on the banks of the Cape Fear River by a Scots family, originally from Greenock, who had rice plantations, and had been slave-owners of a considerable scale " before the war " which freed the slaves. Made aware of my deep, absorbing interest in the whole racial question, my host took me on his private launch up the river to the plantation which spreads away on three sides from the old Colonial house facing the river.

It was just like a page out of *Uncle Tom's Cabin*, the beautiful old house, with its dignified exterior and its wealth of treasures within, discreetly removed from the negro quarters down on the edge of the swamps. The whole atmosphere of the place interested and yet depressed me. Some miasma from the past seemed to have that queer Southern picture in its grip. Yet the people gathered together for me to say a word to, seemed a happy, well-cared-for crowd. Race consciousness possibly had not yet penetrated to the rice fields.

I had heard a good deal from Washington house-wives of the change that had come over their negro servants, once the most perfect in the world, whether regarded from the standpoint of devotion, loyalty, or efficiency. In the cities they had organised themselves into Clubs and Unions, where they met regularly for discussion of their immediate status and affairs and the future for their race lying ahead. In consequence, so I was told, the attitude of the servants had become more arrogant and less re-spectful, and race consciousness having developed the passion for justice and equality which is inherent alike in black and white, though it may be repressed and almost extinguished by oppression.

The negroes are very emotional and religious. Apparently the old Scots slave-owner (strange racial alliance) had salved his conscience by pandering to that side of the negroes' character; building churches or meeting-houses every few miles. These queer little tabernacles, all of which had their full complement of worshippers every Sunday, were an outstanding feature of the landscape.

A description of one negro meeting will suffice, as it was typical of all.

It was held in one of the coloured schools. My hostess took me to the door in her car but declined to accompany me farther. "No, no," she said, with a smile. "*We* don't go to nigger meetings."

I did not realise till that moment how complete is the cleavage between black and white in the southern states. It was really an event for a white woman to address a negro meeting. In consequence, they had turned out in force. It was a splendid meeting. I never had a more interested or responsive audience. Very emotional, my descriptions of war conditions, more especially the destruction of our home by Zeppelins, reduced them to tears. They promised everything in the way of food conservation, and I believe the appeal really did bring some result. But, of course, on minds so emotional impressions are necessarily and inevitably evanescent.

Even those who have never been down South,

but who may have paid a casual visit to Haarlem, the negro city inside the city of New York, must feel that the negro is one of America's greatest if not indeed its very greatest problem.

With the growth and spread of education, race consciousness is being rapidly developed, and it is not easy to see how racial conflict of the most serious kind can be avoided in the coming years.

.   .   .   .

After two months of this very strenuous work, it became necessary for me to return home to see to my own people and affairs.

But I had not been home very long when Mr. Hoover cabled to our Government asking if I could be lent to the American Government for a further spell of service for them.   After some consideration, I agreed to go back.

The second campaign was in some respects more wonderful than the first.   It was certainly carried on under very different conditions.   The American Administration provided me with a member of the Secret Service, who arranged everything, travelled with me, and relieved me of every duty, except that of speaking.

It was a less adventurous journey in consequence. One's initiative was not called into play.   But on the other hand there were no lapses, no wasted or futile journeys.   The schedule was worked out according to plan.

This would seem to be the place to insert some of the testimonials received as to the nature and the

value of the work I did for my own Government
and the American Administration at that time.

From Mr. Herbert Hoover.

UNITED STATES FOOD ADMINISTRATION,
WASHINGTON,
April 25, 1918.

MY DEAR MRS. BURNETT SMITH,—I have just
heard that you have been called back to England,
and regret that I shall not have the opportunity
of seeing you again in Washington so as to thank
you personally for the very great service which you
have rendered during the past few weeks, in giving
the Food Message throughout this country.

The splendid and moving appeal you made here
in Washington at the meeting of the State Food
Administrators in March caused all present to
request that they be allowed the privilege of having
you visit their respective States, and from those
cities that were fortunate enough to be included in
your trip have come the most flattering replies,
thanking the Food Administration for the opportunity of hearing you.

I would be particularly thankful if you would
express to Colonel Buchan our appreciation of his
kindness in making your visit possible.

I would be specially pleased if, after your return
to your own country, you might find it possible to
return here and place us further under obligation
to you for your services in bringing home to the
American people the necessity for Food Conserva-

tion, and emphasising our privilege of assisting the Allies at this time in our common cause.

I trust you will allow me to express my personal thanks to you, and also my wish that you may have a safe and comfortable return to your own country.— Faithfully yours,   HERBERT HOOVER.

UNITED STATES FOOD ADMINISTRATION,
WASHINGTON,
April —, 1918.

DEAR MRS. BURNETT SMITH,—I am very sorry to hear that you are leaving immediately for London.

On the other hand, I cannot complain in view of the very fine service you have done for us.

I think it would be a good plan if we could have five or six women of your own abilities and experience to come to the United States and convey the same message, and I am wondering if, in addition to your own future at a later date, you would not discuss and answer this proposition with the friends in England.—Yours faithfully,
HERBERT HOOVER.

From Colonel John Buchan, Director, Ministry of Information.

NORFOLK STREET, STRAND, LONDON,
May 30, 1918.

DEAR MRS. BURNETT SMITH,—I am directed by the Minister of Information to express to you his very great gratitude for the admirable work you have done for your country in America, and his congratulations upon the remarkable success with which your work was attended. We have heard of your speaking from every kind of source, and always in the terms of the highest praise.

We are very glad to know that you would be willing to return to America for further service, should circumstances make it desirable.—Yours very sincerely, JOHN BUCHAN.

UNITED STATES FOOD ADMINISTRATION,
WASHINGTON,
Feb. 10, 1919.

Sir William Goode,
British Ministry of Food,
London, England.

MY DEAR SIR WILLIAM,—In Mr. Rickard's temporary absence from America, I take pleasure in writing you a personal letter to advise you how greatly we appreciated the visit of Mrs. Burnett Smith to this country. Coming as she did after the signing of the Armistice, our original plan to have her make a second campaign in the interests of food conservation had to be slightly changed.

It seemed to us that the opportunity was ripe to tell our American audiences something of Britain's part in the war. This she did, with great eloquence and most splendid results, and we of the Food Administration here feel that we owe a great debt of gratitude to your Ministry for making it possible for her to come. We sincerely trust that when she arrives home, she will be in good health and have stood the hardships of her trip with no harm to herself.

We have received a very large number of letters from various places expressing the high appreciation of the organisations and towns she was able to visit.—Yours faithfully,

(Signed)   H. ALEXANDER SMITH.

From Sir Henry Babington Smith,
British War Mission.

MUNSEY BUILDING,
WASHINGTON, D.C.,
January 27, 1919.

DEAR MRS. BURNETT SMITH,—I am very sorry not to have had an opportunity of meeting you at Mrs. Hennen Jennings', as I have heard much about your work and should have liked to hear more about it from yourself.   I know that it has been very arduous and of the greatest value ; and I hope that your present visit to America may not be the last.

I quite agree with what you say as to the critical nature of the present time for the relations of the two countries, and you are probably right in thinking that its importance is not fully realised in London. The change from war to peace necessarily brings with it some change in the methods which are appropriate, and the question of future arrangements is under consideration on the other side.

16

You will probably have opportunities, when you reach London, of representing the position as you see it, and I hope that you will make use of them. From the wide experience that you have had, I do not doubt that your views will carry weight.

I fear that I shall not be in New York again before the 29th, and there is not time now for you to return to Washington ; but if by any chance your ship is delayed, please let me know. I shall probably be in New York on Friday next.—Believe me, Yours sincerely,

(Signed)   H. BABINGTON SMITH.

From Sir William Goode.

BRITISH MINISTRY OF FOOD,
HOTEL MAJESTIC, PARIS,
February 17, 1919.

DEAR MRS. BURNETT SMITH,—Many thanks for your letter of the 12th, and still more thanks for your extremely interesting letter of January 24th.

I am discussing with The Powers that be in Paris what you say in your letter of January 24th. I am particularly anxious to see you as soon as I return.

I am extremely grateful for the splendid work you have done. I saw Mr. Rickard here and he said you excelled yourself, than which there can be no higher praise.—Yours sincerely,

WILLIAM GOODE.

Mrs. Burnett Smith,
   Cecil House,
      Hertford.

From Colonel Buchan.

(*Copy.*)

DEAR SIR WILLIAM GOODE,—I quite agree with
you that Mrs. Burnett Smith ought to get a C.B.E.
for the splendid work she did in America. I cannot
put her up, as our Ministry is dissolved. So much
of her work was done for you, I shall only be too
glad to co-operate.

From all accounts, it would not be easy to over-
estimate the good she did.—Yours sincerely,

JOHN BUCHAN.

———

No decorations, however, were forthcoming, much
to my relief, though my family, who knew what the
work had cost me, were not of the same mind.

I have never been a wire-puller, and the wholesale
distribution of war decorations became such a
public scandal that it was more dignified, if not
even more distinguished, not to have been offered
one. My reward was in the unique and priceless
opportunity afforded me to render what was acknowledged to be a genuine bit of war service. It
was acknowledged and recognised by those on the
spot. Even the British Bureau of Information in
New York became very respectful to me, and
solicitous about my welfare. A wonderful chapter
of experience was added to my book of life, and I
have never ceased to thank God for it.

———

It was when the Labour Government was in
power that I received later the *C.B.E.* for " literary

and public services." I accepted it without undue elation, chiefly because the one who would have been proudest of it had passed out and on.

I *did* prize, however, the Queen Elizabeth Medal, which I received from the King of the Belgians, immediately the war ended, for the small services I had been able to tender to the group of his subjects we had cared for in Hertford.

CHAPTER TWENTY-THREE

RECONSTRUCTION—POLITICS

THE business of reconstruction is always beset with difficulties. For a whole year our door had been closed to patients, owing to the substitute being called up, and the impossibility of finding any one to fill his place. The practice was scattered among the other doctors, and it was, of course, a difficult and delicate business getting the patients all back. People, especially when they are ill, dislike being handed about from one man to another. That is why there is something wrong with the sale of medical practices. Some other way should be found of transferring interests. Yet, when one man's energy and personality have built up a large practice, it would seem unreasonable for him to walk out without compensation. The best solution is a partnership.

When we came back to Hertford it seemed a changed world, the position savouring a little of the days when we squatted hopefully in a new neighbourhood and waited for results. It did not take long, however, for my Doctor was greatly beloved, especially by the working folks. Sprung from them himself, he understood their needs, their difficulties, and their outlook on life. Quite often, during his absence on war service, people I didn't know would dash up to me in the street, demanding the latest news about their dear Doctor. It was then I learned that they called him " the friend of the poor."

It is a proud title which thousands of hard-working general practitioners have earned, and will continue to earn, unless the healing art becomes a Robot of the State, or so commercialised that its pristine flavour will be gone. My husband not only healed their bodies, he made their wills, helped them to settle their children in life, umpired their quarrels, and gave them good advice on every conceivable subject. I gather from what I hear that this rich, rewarding side of the medical profession is less common than it was.

The practice was built up again, but Jim reckoned that his war service had cost him at least two thousand pounds. Not that he grudged it. Like all voluntary service, undertaken in the right spirit, it had enriched his life. But he was not the man he had been, nor possessed the stamina for broken nights and continuous work. So we began to consider the idea of getting a partner.

Again the housing problem was the lion in the path. The war had stopped all building operations, and there was no sort of accommodation available in the neighbourhood, except the North House, which was standing gaunt and empty, though it had been repaired at our expense. After much consultation we decided to acquire the remainder of the lease and move in, thus freeing Cecil House for the young partner.

I don't know whether it was a good move. We dropped money on it, as we had dropped it on most of our undertakings. Somehow we had never been obsessed by money, nor had any desire to amass it. Its only value to us was what it could buy in the way of beauty and comfort, and the help it enabled us to give to others.

The lovely garden had speedily been restored by Nature to the jungle. Weeds and nettles six feet high had choked the herbaceous borders, and waving grasses had destroyed the lawns. But some good spade work and George's indomitable spirit quickly restored it to something like its former glory.

Our lives appeared to move in cycles—five and two, the numbers which ordered our lives. We have never been longer than five years in any house. We were only four in the restored house.

The partnership was as successful as the majority of partnerships. It is a delicate and difficult connection always. The old patients want the old doctor, and an eager, enthusiastic young man is apt to regard his older colleague as a back number. My husband was a tireless worker, who had always sacrificed himself, and frequently his home, to the claims of his practice. It was sometimes a bone of contention between us. The younger generation won't do that. Our partner liked his days off for golf and other things, and took them when so minded, and all was changed.

I took up most of the threads of life again without difficulty, as things became more normal. Very gradually we began to realise, not only the awful cost of war, but its deadly aftermath. In the first burst of relief and joy over the cessation of the fighting we imagined our sorrows were all over. Actually they were only beginning, and some of the horrors of peace, bar the actual bloodshed, have exceeded those of war. Yet there are to be found even yet advocates of war, and the poor League of Nations which, properly upheld and allowed to function, could really make an end of strife has fallen into sad disrepute.

About this time I began to take a more active interest in politics. It was an accident, or rather, at first a matter of pure sentiment. I had watched for some time with warm and sympathetic interest the gallant stand made in the House by my old friend Sir Donald Maclean and his little band since the breakup of the Coalition. I was not taking any particular side in that fight, though I had been a Liberal all my life, since the days when Gladstone first stirred my girlish imagination. It was the human side of it all that interested me, and finally I wrote and asked whether there was anything I could do to help.

There seemed to be plenty of work for any one willing to do it, and I was soon on the speaker's list. I have never pretended to be a politician.

I have not got that cast of mind. Party politics do not interest me in the least. What does interest me is the broad basis of humanity, and what Liberal ideas, in the wider, not the party sense, can do to salve some of the ills of our time. I have never hidden either my views or my limitations. It is rather distressing, however, when charged with a message representing the views of your own side, to suddenly see with appalling clearness the other party's side. It has quite often disconcerted me. However, I have done a lot of good work for the Cause I have had so long at heart ; and though I may not have been able to achieve a telling political speech, to the confusion of the opposing camp, I have most certainly advocated Liberalism with all the eloquence at my command.

I have also done a good deal of the spade work. I was even induced, through some strange concatenation of circumstances, to stand as Liberal candidate for the Maryhill division of Glasgow in the campaign of 1922 when the Labour Party swept the board.

The day after the newspapers had announced that my name had been added to the list of Liberal candidates, I met Sir Benjamin Faudel-Phillips in Fore Street, and we stopped to talk. Pretending to look very stern, he said :

" Is this true, that you are standing as a Liberal candidate ? "

I replied that it was quite true, and that I was going to Glasgow next day ; whereupon he shook his head and said sadly : " It's a great strain on friendship." Then we both laughed and concluded that our friendship would stand it.

I realised at a very early stage in the campaign that I hadn't an earthly chance, and that it was a constituency no woman should have been asked to fight. I did the best I could, putting in three weeks' strenuous work, speaking daily at several meetings, receiving endless deputations and committees, and, incidentally, acquiring increased respect for all who are willing to go through such a treadmill, either for their own or their country's sake. Considering my elemental knowledge of politics and general inexperience, I was considered to have put up a fairly good show. I wasn't ready witted enough for the hecklers, though I got a lot of fun out of them.

They were all very kind and friendly to me ; while Helen Fraser was getting her platforms smashed up in Govan, they treated me with perfect courtesy. Of course the strenuous opposition she received was a tribute to her political ability and her fearlessness in attack. I attacked nobody. In that respect I was a poor candidate.

The campaign had its humours. An old friend of mine, Mrs. Anton of Kidderminster, a magistrate and prominent worker in her own town, came up to do canvassing for me. She brought home all sorts of queer stories at the close of the day's work. One afternoon she climbed a steep stair to a landing where there were two doors. When she knocked at one, both opened, and two heads appeared. When she explained her errand, number one lady

said cheerfully : "Oh yes, I'm votin' for her."
Whereupon number two said truculently : "I'm
no' gaunna vote for her."

Great indignation on the part of number one,
who immediately threw out this ultimatum :

"Weel, if you're no' gaun to vote for her, ye can
buy yer ain *People's Friend* after this."

The *People's Friend* figured largely in the campaign. One night Effie, waiting in the car outside
the gate of the school where I was speaking, over-
heard two small urchins discussing the notice board.

"Wha's this Annie Swan ? " queried one.

"Oh, d'ye no' ken ? She's the *People's Friend.*"

I liked that, and I hope it was true.

At several meetings I had been followed by a
very truculent female, who bombarded me with
questions, till I got exasperated and silenced her,
saying other people must have a chance, but that
if she had anything further to say to me, she could
come round to the anteroom after the meeting.
She came, and I asked the Committee to withdraw.
Then I walked up to her, put my hand on her
shoulder, and asked her what it was all about, and
that though we saw things from different angles,
surely there was no need for her to be so disagreeable
about it. To my surprise she burst into tears and
explained that she was sent out by her group to
do this at meetings. We discussed things quite
amicably, and her parting words were :

"I'll be there the morn's night doin' the same
thing, but you'll ken I'm a'richt inside."

One afternoon, in a slum area, I was talking to a very poor woman. I have never forgotten her words:
" Ah, weel," she said, " I dinna understand it a'. We'll vote for onybody that will mak' us better."

It sums up the hope and the scope of the average voter's mind, and is part of the psychology of every Parliamentary election.

In spite of my inadequate equipment, which I am quite sure must often have discouraged my devoted band of workers, I polled over 6000 votes, which in the circumstances was a mild kind of personal triumph. I wish to leave it on record how courteous, even chivalrous, my Labour opponents were to me throughout the entire campaign. Of course I never attacked them. My job was to present my own programme, which I did to the very best of my ability. It was a three-cornered contest, and I can't say that the Conservative candidate showed me the same courtesy or consideration.

When the poll was declared, I asked the victorious candidate, Mr. James Muir, to what he attributed his overwhelming success. His reply was enlightening and a comment on the slacker Liberal tactics:

" Thirty years' intensive work and training at the street corners."

Since then I have been more or less in politics, doing a good deal of speaking, and helping to get big meetings together for more highly equipped defenders of the faith. It has brought me, of course, into contact with all the Liberal leaders. I have a very happy memory of the late Lord Oxford.

We had gathered at Dumfries for a great meeting to close, I think, the Annual Conference of the Scottish Liberal Federation. We had some big guns that night—Mr. Asquith, Lady Bonham Carter, Sir Donald Maclean, and Dr. Hunter in the chair. For some reason or another the meeting was incredibly dull. It went on getting deader and deader, till one might have thought the whole audience asleep. It was easy to see that unless something could be done, the meeting was a failure. I had to propose one of the resolutions, but first I had to awaken the audience. And I did. I don't know how exactly, unless because I knew the psychology of Scottish audiences from A to Z. I got them rocking with laughter, and when the meeting was over, Mr. Asquith put his hand on my shoulder and said :

" My dear, you are an artist. Without you we were damned." He spoke with feeling, and my eyes filled with tears.

———

I had some correspondence at various times with the late Lord Rosebery, one of the brightest jewels in the Liberal crown.

One of his letters, now before me, written by his own hand, contains a mild rebuke which in these days of rabid nationalism may not be without interest. The rebuke was publicly administered in large block letters on the envelope which came through the post from Dalmeny to Kinghorn, a few miles distant.

It appears that I had been guilty of the unforgivable sin of putting the objectionable letters N.B. on my notepaper. Thus did Lord Rosebery recall me to a sense of my fall from grace. His envelope was addressed thus :

> *Mrs. Burnett Smith*
> *The Anchorage*
> *Kinghorn*
> *SCOTLAND.*

The last letter I received from him, also written in his own hand, came from Rosebery, where he was living in seclusion after his adored son was killed in action. I must not transcribe it here. It is too sacred. But I gathered from it that he had sustained a mortal blow.

He was a strange aloof personality, understood by very few.

Sir William Robertson Nicoll often spoke of him, speculating about the inhibitions which had arrested what ought to have been a more glorious career. Even so, he left his mark on his time, and will never be forgotten. I remember yet the thrill one night at the Lambeth Baths, where I had gone by invitation to hear him make a great political speech. Apart from its political significance, it was a rare treat to hear these perfect periods rounded off by the golden voice.

They were giants on political platforms in these days. The Dynasty would appear to be extinct.

Among the friendships which have come to me through political life, I value none more highly than that accorded to me by the late Marquess of Aberdeen and his gifted, wonderful wife.

To have been received by " We Twa " as a guest at Cromar, to have shared intimate talk of the great days of Liberalism is to have acquired a new reverence for the dignity of life, for the sanctity and beauty of the marriage tie, for the goodness and simplicity of noble minds attuned to a common purpose—*i.e.* tireless service for the good of others. We who were associated with Lady Aberdeen on the Women's Council, which was only a small part of her world-wide and beneficent service for humanity, often marvelled and sometimes were rebuked by her selfless devotion.

Taking them all in all, we shall not soon, if ever, look upon their like again.

Like all true Liberals, Lord Aberdeen deplored and condemned the tactics of the breakers who put selfish and narrow aims in front, not behind, the Cause. To him there were only Liberals ; and labels and tags exasperated him. Something of his private conviction about these things is revealed in this letter.

HOUSE OF CROMAR,
Sat. Midnight or a " wee bit ayont "
maybe.

V. DEAR MRS. BURNETT SMITH,—I have just finished, with ever growing interest and enjoyment, *The Shore Beyond.* And now is the moment for offer-

ing my share of warm thanks and congratulation.
I am often told that my letters are " ower lang,"
so that shall suffice meanwhile. I speak of share,
because, of course, the grateful thanks of the actual
recipient of the gift are to follow. But I calmly
annexed the book before she could look at it, she
having returned from a busy and necessary absence
in London and Dublin, fighting a bad cold, which
has troubled her all week.

The Fife election was a disappointment, but you
must be glad that you once more did your bit for
Liberalism.

As to this absurd cult of Simonite, etc., it gives me
a sense of nausea, for it is simply a part of that
deplorable self-centred line which has been so much
the bane of Liberalism.

One would like to think that Sir J. S. himself
would discourage it. The latest example of that
imposture appeared in our local press to-day, viz.
" Samuelite."

That's a calumny. Sir Herbert has never been
anything else than a Liberal in fact and name. But
I must stop this harangue, and return to the more
congenial topic of your latest book.

I feel increasingly its wonderful and sustained
freshness—*inter alia*—and so again congratulation
and affectionate thanks.—As always,

ABERDEEN AND TEMAIR.

Some little time later I happened to be having
tea at Churt with Mr. Lloyd George and his family.

As I sat there listening to his wizard voice, watching the play of his mobile features, quite aware of his personal charm, I asked myself how and why this man, to whom the country and the world owe so much, should have rent a great political party from top to bottom, and managed to alienate beyond all hope of recall, thousands of good men and true, who were once proud to own his leadership.

I thought I had found the key to the riddle that day, but as it might quite easily prove a wrong or ill-fitting key, I will leave it in the door.

.   .   .   .

The future of Liberalism ?   I wonder !

If by some mysterious process of evolution, born of the tremendous epoch on which we have entered, it should cease to function under the old name and banner, that will not mean that it is dead or dying, or that its work is done.   Far otherwise.

A living force, its faith embodying all that is best in human idealism and effort, it will continue its vitalising and beneficent mission.

I am proud to have been associated. even in so small a degree, with its active service.

CHAPTER TWENTY-FOUR

AUTUMN

WHILE I was outwardly busy with all these activities, I kept an unsleeping eye on my home and my husband's health.

I knew that he was failing, and that sooner or later, probably sooner, he must slacken off or retire. These were words for which he had little use, frequently saying he would die in harness, preferably on his feet.

The decline was mercifully gradual, but on the day when he came down from the Hospital saying he would not operate any more, I knew that the limit had been set.

One of the trials of advancing years is that our friends and comrades begin to drop like leaves from the autumnal trees.

He deeply felt the death of Sir William Robertson Nicoll, whose medical adviser he had been so long. They had great tussles during these years, for Nicoll was a difficult patient. His constitution was frail, and he openly defied almost every known law of health, yet managed to turn out work in measure which would have shamed many in perfect health, and to live to pass the allotted span.

Open windows were his pet aversion. Jim had a tale about him. It happened one day when the atmosphere of his bed-sitting-room (which latterly he had to use more than his magnificent library) was more than usually charged with tobacco smoke.

" Fresh air ! Fresh air ! " he shouted. " No, *sir*. It's an invention of the devil. More people have been killed by fresh air than by any other disease. If I ever live to have any leisure, I shall certainly employ it in writing an exhaustive treatise on the evils of fresh air."

We had no doubt at all that the war reduced both his health and his stamina. He felt it deeply and poignantly.

Through his close intimacy with Lloyd George he was aware of most that went on behind the scenes during these desperate years, and could he have been induced to write his impressions on them, a book of extraordinary and quite unique interest would have been the result. But he was never inclined for that, and indeed talked very little about it. The horror and futility of it all had entered like iron into his soul. Readers of the *British Weekly* found from week to week not only the usual comfort in its pages, but a strange assurance that the war notes were infinitely better informed, and far ahead of the majority published even in the daily papers.

He seemed to know things before they happened. He never faltered in his admiration for, and

absolute belief in, Lloyd George, whom he considered to have been the saviour of his country in
a crisis which other men were not strong enough to
grasp or handle.

Another old friend of Jim's, Sir Watson Cheyne,
passed out of our immediate ken about that time,
having suddenly thrown up everything, and gone
off for good to his island home in the far north.
He was a great surgeon and an intimate friend ; he
often came down to us on Sundays to have a brief
rest, and smoke the pipe of peace.   All his life he
had been a stand-by to my husband, giving his
priceless services often to his poorer patients without
fee or reward, except the frequent blessing of
grateful hearts.

" When winter comes " to men they have to make
greater surrenders than women have to make.   Somehow they have fewer resources, and if they happen to
be cut off drastically from strenuous outdoor sports
are often bored and at a loss.   Household cares,
the hundred-and-one infinitesimal jobs which can
fill a woman's hands from morning till night, even
when health and strength have declined, are often
her salvation.

The planning and making of new curtains or
loose covers, changing the rooms, thinking out some
entirely new outfit, either for herself or somebody
else, can fill up many an empty space.   On countless occasions in my own life such homely, but oh,
how important ! tasks have averted a crisis.

A woman said to me one day :

"When I'm desperate I just up an' do a big washing. It's the cure."

Well, men are cut off from that brand of cure, and unless they are readers and have their minds filled with good material, they are sadly at a loss. My husband was a great reader, stealing many hours from sleep. He was always abreast of his profession in study, but it did not, and never could, take the place of active service among the human beings he loved. It was only a substitute, and he chafed at the restricted life he saw unrolling in front. The result was frayed nerves, uncertain tempers, and difficult days.

I began quietly to make plans for the future. We had long decided that, when our work, if not actually finished, should necessarily be curtailed and changed, we would go back to Scotland, where all our relatives lived and with which we had so many dear associations. But we had no home there. The war occupation of the Anchorage had estranged us from it. It was so knocked about, within and without, that we were glad to sell it, at a loss, as usual, and part with most of the furniture. I shall never forget that dreadful day when, after all the pantechnicon vans had moved away from the gate, and I locked the door and turned away to walk the three miles between Kinghorn and Kirkcaldy to catch a train. I was quite alone, and the tears I shed on that bleak highway were some of the bitterest in my life.

My sister Janet, who used to make a home for

us there, had been living in turn with each one of
the family. She was six months with us in Hertford, getting treatment for the serious illness which
ultimately removed her from our circle. She had
to have a leg amputated, and never did any one
face the disabled life more gallantly. She even got
well enough to feel that she wanted a little home of
her own again, so one was found in Kinghorn, so
arranged that with very little help she could manage
it herself, and there she lived for some happy years
until her death.

We decided to look for a new home, and Effie and
I made various pilgrimages to Scotland, inspecting
many houses ; but the kind we wanted were all,
just then, being offered at quite prohibitive prices.
That has been our luck always—to sell in the
cheapest market, and buy in the dearest. It
indicates some lack in worldly wisdom, if nothing
else.

At last we found Bandrum, a small mansion-
house, set snugly at the base of a sunny hill in West
Fife, looking towards the sea. We loved Fife,
though we were prepared to go anywhere else, if
the right house turned up.

Bandrum was four miles from Dunfermline, on
the Saline road, and had the most lovely old walled
garden and twenty-four acres of woodlands, an
ideal spot for rest or refreshment, though a little
remote for some other purposes. It certainly
created domestic difficulties, such as we had never
known. The distance from pictures and shops,

Photo: *Francis Inglis.*

BANDRUM, WHERE Dr. BURNETT SMITH DIED

and the long, dark avenue did not appeal to young
servants, and I tasted for the first time the discomfort of inefficient service and ever-changing faces
in my house.

We carried back such a good report of the place
that Jim went up to see it, and wired that he had
bought it. It wanted a lot of doing to it, central
heating and lighting installed, but it was ready for
us for a summer holiday, in fact we had two summers
there before we left England. Our departure could
not be accomplished in a hurry.

His half of the practice had to be disposed of,
and a house found for the purchaser. We knew
that it would be useless to expect any young man
to take over the North House, with its basement and
other inconveniences, and the great garden which
required two men to keep it. One day Jim had a
brain wave. The kitchen garden, about half an
acre in extent, had a frontage to the street and was
entirely cut off from the house by a wall on two
sides. He decided to build a small, labour-saving
house on the site, and try to dispose of the property
in two lots.

All was accomplished according to plan, and the
day came when we once more turned our faces to
the north, this time for good. There were many
sore hearts in the pleasant little town—ours included
—but no spectacular farewell.

He had bought a new car ; it was brought to the
door in the afternoon, and though he had never
seen it before, we drove away in it, four hundred

miles, to coveted rest and peace. That was so like
him. He had no hesitation about taking any kind
of risk. Fear was not in him. George Cook sat
grimly in the back seat, having agreed to go north
and see us " in." The two others had gone by
train—but we were not able to keep them. It was
too far from home, they said. I think they regretted it afterwards. We certainly did, and though
in time we were happy to get some one like them,
not a casual help, but a stayer and a friend, they
have never been forgotten.

We settled in happily. Friends and relations
gathered about us. Donald and Mary from Aber-
foyle, John and Margaret from the Tolbooth Manse,
my eldest sister's family from Kennoway. But
you cannot spend thirty-five happy years anywhere
without feeling the wrench of parting, and our roots,
especially Jim's, had been sunk deep in English
soil. The life was pleasant at Bandrum, and its
master took much joy in recreating the beautiful
garden without hurt to its old world charm.

The second summer we took a trip to America
to pay a number of visits to the friends I had made
during my war service. It was a delightful, memor-
able trip, on which there was leisure and opportunity, entirely denied to me before, to see some of
the beauties of that marvellous country. All the
while, however, I was aware of a strange, secret fear
of the same kind which had obsessed me before the
war. It lay on me like the shadow of impending
doom. As we were whirled from one marvellous

THE TERRACE WALK, BANDRUM

experience to another, daily witnesses to the overwhelming prosperity, the wild extravagance, the headlong rush for pleasure, I was afraid. Perhaps it was the contrast between the New World and the Old, still suffering and groaning under the wounds of war and the dangers of peace, which made me say again and again : " This can't last. These cities remind me of Babylon and Nineveh and Tyre. There is bound to be a judgment."

Our old proverb, " The fu' cup is ill to carry," was never more justified and exemplified than that summer we spent in the United States. And sure enough the boom did not last.

A woman said to me one day : " Do you know, I never in my life have wanted a thing I couldn't get ? "

She stared at me when, instead of congratulating her, I said I was sorry for her. There is no doubt in my mind at all that life is not meant to be lived like that. We are here for some purpose ; quite frequently possibly so obscure that we don't discover it until it is too late to repair the omissions or the commissions in which we have indulged. Moreover, a life lived on the hilltops knows nothing of the quiet shades in the valley, which are even more necessary to growth than the glaring sunshine.

America will emerge from her Gethsemane stronger and better and richer in the best sense than she has yet been.

Our life at home moved on quietly. Jim took up

some public work, of which he had had much experience in England. The Education Authority interested him enormously, and he greatly enjoyed the comradeship of his colleagues. There is a side of a man's life no woman can touch or share, and she is a fool if she thinks she can. I have known several wives of the possessive brand, who have even boasted that they were all in all to their husbands, who desired no companionship but theirs. There is a good old Scotch word, not perhaps used by the best people, but as I am only a plain working woman I'll set it down—" Blethers ! "

I was as busy as ever, opening bazaars, speaking in support of good causes all over the country, and occasionally appearing on political platforms. My literary work, of course, was first and foremost, and never, surely, had it been done in such delectable circumstances. My study commanded a magnificent view right down to the sea, and was a complete sun-trap. I was obliged, in self-defence, to set my desk at an angle as far from the window as possible. Sunny vistas are not favourable to desk work. They are rivals and competitors. Then the birds ! I could write pages about the concerts they provided for me in the early mornings, when I would creep, before the household was astir, to start my day's work. I always had just one long look from the window, to watch for a minute or so the antics of the rabbits on the dewy lawns and the joyous movements of the birds as they carolled from bough to bough. Great mornings, in which my heart

Photo: *Francis Inglis.*

Dr. BURNETT SMITH
1927, YEAR OF HIS DEATH

joined with the rest of creation in a pæan of thanksgiving and praise.

We had many visitors at Bandrum—friends from far and near, from Hertford and even London. George Doran, the American publisher, St. John Ervine, Alice Head, Claire Leighton, the child we used to know, who has developed into a famous artist in woodcuts, Lady Robertson Nicoll, Grange and Mildred, Elystan and Connie. Also Effie's war comrades—again and again. They all loved it, and wanted to come back.

But slowly, almost imperceptibly, the clouds began to gather again. In one short year we lost three out of our circle—two sisters greatly beloved, and a favourite nephew, who died untimely, after a distinguished career in medicine and in war service. My husband's health was steadily declining, and in May 1927 the end came.

He had no prolonged illness, for which I was thankful, for he could not have borne it. During these desperate last days, when I kept vigil in the night watches, I was profoundly aware of the awful loneliness of the human soul. Even while he was still with me, in a sense I had lost him. He had gone where neither my love nor my care could reach him.

He was beautiful in life, but in death there was upon his face a majesty which laid a hush on my riven heart and dried my tears.

He often called himself a fighter—now, having laid his armour down—he had come not only to ineffable peace, but to some radiant shore on which sorrow, frustration, defeat, have no place.

.   .   .   .

We laid him on the windy hill at Kinghorn beside the son he had so loved.

In death they are not divided.

CHAPTER TWENTY-FIVE

THE WIFE AND THE CAREER

I HAVE quite frequently wished to write an article under the above heading, especially after perusing the effusions of other people, some of whom obviously had no experience either of wifehood or a career. But always there was a hesitancy about setting down what must of necessity be intimate conclusions concerning oneself and another.

However, now that is all over, and I have nearly half a century of experience behind me, I may be permitted a few reflections on the subject. It will help if we start with the platitude that the happiest wives, like the happiest nations, have no history. When they marry, they merge themselves in their husbands' interests and in their homes, and the world hears not of them ; is even unaware that the contribution they are making to the common weal may be of infinitely more value than many careers.

It is impossible to tackle this thorny theme without some generalisation on the subject of matrimony.

It has been much in the limelight of late, harried and tormented, turned inside out, put violently in

its place, threatened with weird improvements—
save the mark—and even with ultimate extinction.
But in an unstable, shattered world, it is one of the
things which, though shaken, will remain, because
it is not of human ordination. Since the beginning
of time, when " man and woman created He them,"
and set the solitary together in families, Home has
been the Mecca of the great human dream.

Though it may be assaulted from without or
betrayed by those within, it will never be thrown on
the scrap-heap. Each new generation will give it
welcome, accepting its fulfilment and its limitations with high and happy confidence. They will,
like their forebears in the married estate, have their
grievances and their disappointments, sometimes
even they will be driven to the point of desperate
wonder that they should have been such fools as
to run their necks into the noose.   There is a fearful
permanency about the marriage-tie.

You can never return from that high adventure
as you may return from other adventures, without
carrying its indelible impress on mind and heart.
Even when tragic disillusionment summons the law
to break or set aside the bond, you may imagine
yourself unmarried, only to find that you are not.
You may be, in the letter, perhaps, but in the spirit
you never get away.

To return to the average marriage which, thank
God, holds to the end, the acid tests are exaspera-
tion and excessive boredom. I heard the wife of a
distinguished divine say once : " It is possible to

love your husband dearly and yet to wish, quite often, to throw him out of the window."

Husbands, as well as wives, have these exasperated spells. Once, at a Women's Luncheon Club in Leeds, when I had been asked to speak on Matrimony, the audience seemed rather startled when I propounded my conviction that it is quite possible to live happily with a man with whom you hardly ever agree about anything. I hastened to add to " agree to differ " was the only platform from which such a feat could be accomplished. There are, however, several ways of agreeing to differ, some of them more disastrous than open disagreement. If the compromisers adopt a lofty air of superiority, their last end will probably be worse than their first.

In our case, though we started young and fair, well equipped with love and faith and a common determination to make a success of our dual life, we had various handicaps to contend with. We were both strong characters, holding definite opinions about most things, seeing life from entirely different angles, moreover we had both quick and fiery tempers. Disciplinary measures are necessary for the control of these conflicting handicaps, and only love is capable of contributing the dynamic force. We had sufficient to carry us through.

I confess I have never been able to call up any admiration for, or even belief in, the vaunted felicity of the married couples who present themselves at Dunmow to receive their haloes in the form of a flitch of bacon. Two people who can live together, year in, and year out, without a hint of discord, a single cloud on their marble brows, or "a little rift" within their matrimonial lute, do not commend themselves to me as supermen and superwomen, but only dull ones. I think the flitch could be more appropriately awarded to those who are able to hold to the bond through years of stress and toil, who have their scraps, their silences and estrangements, who bear the scars of battle on their hearts, but who cling together because love holds them in dear comradeship and community of interest. We could have put in for such a prize, for we both earned it.

Now, the husband whose wife is in any way in the public eye, whether as writer, painter, scientist, teacher, or politician, is in a position slightly different from that of other husbands. He finds himself not the sole, sometimes not even the principal, star in the firmament, and being what he is, the average male finds that a hard nut to crack, sometimes a bitter one. When both husband and wife have careers, it is essential, for domestic peace and harmony, that his should be equal in success and achievement. The chances of happiness are increased and rendered more secure when their work lies along different lines. The risk of any form of jealousy or competition is thus eliminated.

There are cases, of course, of exceptions to this general conclusion, but I cannot help thinking that those who achieve happiness in such circumstances are special people

It quite often happens that the wife, who has a career, puts it before her home. Where the ego is strongly developed, she does not see straight. Lifted up and carried along on the flood-tide of her success and achievement, she minimises her duties and obligations in the humbler and rather less spectacular walks of daily living. I have seen a good many shipwrecks on this hidden reef.

When I hear a woman complaining that the domestic world offers no scope for her genius, or airily dismissing the conduct of a home as something any woman of brains can dispose of in an hour or two, I am filled with a kind of wonder. It is not only a mistake, it is a lie. Neither home-making nor housekeeping can be disposed of in any such casual manner. I realised that at the very outset of my life, and was only able to achieve some success in two worlds, if I may put it like that, at the cost of considerable sacrifice. I never obtruded my writing—it was done mostly in the early morning, while others were asleep. I seldom talked about it, and I gave the most meticulous attention to household affairs and to all the unceasing demands which sets a doctor's house apart from others. I am not pretending that it was easy. Quite the reverse. But it was tremendously worth while. It kept the balance in the home, and the head of the house knew that he *was* its head. So did the outside world.

I am aware that these antiquated notions are not acceptable to this generation, and that the

18

marching feet of modern women are eager to abolish every barrier, and achieve complete equality in every department of life and conduct. They have still Nature to overcome at the last barrier, and the final word will be hers now, as it has always been. The universal cry for personal freedom brings in its train the shirking of responsibility. But there are signs of a reaction setting in, and that the balance of family life, like the balance of trade, bids fair to be restored.

We did our best, but we had our dud days when the curtain threatened to ring down on our happiness. But even when the fret and fever of daily living most irked us, we never thought of parting. We were there for keeps, " for better for worse," and were prepared to stand by our vows. It was all so much for the better that mostly we were full of gratitude and wonder that romance could have lived so long and survived so much.

I have always been profoundly grateful for the help I received in my work from my husband's medical knowledge. It was quite incalculable. I asked him about everything, and received so much wise counsel concerning the probable reactions n some of the more trying situations of life, that it would be quite accurate to say he helped me in that sense to write my books.

I was able, though in far less degree, to be o occasional help to him. For instance, he came in one day and said :

" I can't do any more for poor Mrs. ——. Her

number's up. She's afraid to die. You must go and lift her up."

My intuition about people, too, a sort of mysterious sixth sense which seldom seemed to err, was sometimes of service to him in his public life. He was wonderful about my work—jealous of its quality, eager that it should be recognised and acclaimed.

Never, in all the years we lived together, did he ask how much money I had made or what I had done with it. He earned enough for the upkeep of his home and the family needs. What I made provided the frills and the adventures. We had, from the beginning to the end, separate banking accounts. Nor did he ever seek to influence either my opinions or my actions. A staunch Conservative all his life, he respected the Liberal faith in which I had been reared, and when I went as a candidate to the Maryhill division of Glasgow, he came up and stood by me through the last week of the campaign. How could one forget or minimise a gesture like that ?

On occasion he would complain about my public work calling me so often from home. Once, when we were arguing about it, I said : " But you are so little in the house. You are just like a lodger, who arrives to eat and sleep. What sort of family life is that ? "

He agreed that it was a poor sort, but added, with that queer twinkle in his eye which made short work of my defences :

" But, you see, I like you to be there, in case I might happen to want you."

To the last day of his life, when the relations between men and women came under discussion, he maintained that a man loves only once, and that minor strayings of fancy don't count at all. He never dogmatised about women, though his profession brought him into close contact with them, often in their moments of weakness and stress. No wise man ever does dogmatise about woman. She remains to him, first and last, an enigma, part of the riddle of the universe.

He was a great lover, and though he wrung my heart a thousand times, as I must have wrung his, the bond held inviolate to the end. When a woman can run to her mate, as I often did, when shattered by the stress of life, crying : " Hold me tight— I'm going to pieces ! " there is not much wrong with her matrimonial outfit. He needed no explanation of these minor explosions. He understood.

That is how I have been able to write my love stories, and why I shall go on writing them to the end. A woman whom I was recommending to write love stories, as she had the gift and there is always a market for them, said to me firmly : " You can't write about what you don't believe in." That may be so. In my inner life I have never been faced with that challenge.

And when the long last mile has been traversed, I shall be fain to meet my life's companion of forty-four years again in the " land of morning and perpetual spring."

These lines I found in an old anthology seem to me to sum up the epic of married life as I have known it :

" And though the first sweet sting of love be past,
The sweet that almost venom is, though Youth,
Its tender and extravagant delights,
Pass off. There shall succeed a faithful peace,
Beautiful friendship tried by sun and wind,
Durable from the daily dust of life.
And though with sadder, yet with kinder eyes
We shall behold all frailties, we shall haste
To pardon and with mellowing minds to bless.
Then, though we must grow old, we shall grow old
Together—and he shall not greatly miss
My bloom faded, and waning light of eyes
Too deeply gazed in ever to seem dim.
Nor shall we murmur at nor much regret
The years that gently bend us to the ground.
Endeared by many griefs, by many a jest,
And custom sweet of living side by side,
        Last, we shall descend
Into the natural ground, not without tears.
One must go first, ah, God, one must go first.
After so long, one blow for both were good !
Still, like old friends, glad to have met, we leave
Behind a wholesome memory on the earth."

CHAPTER TWENTY-SIX

THE REWARDS OF AUTHORSHIP (I)

THIS is a tremendous theme, about which there is much confusion, as well as curiosity, in the public mind. There is more loose talk about the rewards of authorship than about almost any other theme in the world. It is always " news " for which the whole world seems to be gasping.

I shall do my best to dissipate some of the fairy tales that have been woven about the earnings of authors. At least, I shall be quite frank about my own.

I have already mentioned, I think, that the only best seller I have ever achieved was *Aldersyde*; which goes on selling in some quarters to this day. For the copyright of *Aldersyde* I received the sum of fifty pounds, and no further payment whatsoever.

I blame nobody for this, least of all the publishers, who took the risk of introducing to the public a new and quite unknown name. They gave me my chance, and in those days, fifty pounds to a penniless girl was a small fortune.

For my second book, *Carlowrie*, I received seventy-five pounds, and for *The Gates of Eden* a hundred, parting with the copyright in each case. I have never been much of a business woman, and though I did not despise the money (far from it—only a fool does that), its only purpose in my estimation was to adorn life and help others.

I came, indeed, to the middle years before I realised the necessity for saving something for the rainy day, my husband setting me the example. Undoubtedly the fairest system is that of royalties, whereby the author shares the responsibility and the risk, as well as the possible returns. I am sure that publishers must lose as well as make enormous sums, for the whole business is a bit of a gamble. The public is a fickle jade who, for no known reason, may acclaim a writer one day, and reject him the next. Writing indeed is, of all professions, the most insecure, and a reputation is as hard, sometimes harder, to uphold than to achieve. Its hazards indeed are extraordinary. An old friend of mind, once a reader to a well-known publishing house, curses himself to this day for having rejected for his firm one of the immortals—to wit, *Treasure Island*.

So inefficient a business woman am I that I have, on occasion, signed an agreement without reading it, clear evidence surely that I required some one to act for me. I had a literary agent for a good many years, one of the most efficient, who, beyond doubt, got me more money, besides saving me all kinds of business negotiations.

But there is no personal tie between author and publisher when business is done through an agent.

After I became established, and knew exactly what my public wanted, the agent seemed superfluous, and I gave him up, not without some regrets. I have never been a best seller, nor have a large library public in the ordinary sense. Libraries like Mudie's and Smith's do not take whole editions of my books, but only a few copies. The Free Libraries, I think, stock some of them more generously, and I have heard from many librarians that they are much in demand. I am sometimes asked how many books I have written. I reply, quite truthfully, that I don't know. I do not feel any particular thrill of pride when I gaze upon them on the shelves. They have served their purpose, and as none of them is likely to prove immortal, their number is a matter of no importance.

I have made a very excellent livelihood by the writing of serial stories, thanks to my happy association with the Dundee firm, with occasional excursions into the magazine world. My public is mainly a serial one, though occasionally, to satisfy some secret hunger in my soul, I have written a book and sent it out, on a voyage of discovery, usually with only modest success.

While we were living at Bandrum, I wrote *The Pendulum*, the history of which may be of some little interest to some readers who have accompanied me thus far along the road I have travelled. After the war, the late Sir Ernest Hodder Williams, who had great respect for my work, kept on urging me to write a story dealing with the effect of the war on family life. I did not particularly want to write such a book, and told him so. I had seen so much of war's deadly aftermath, had been behind the scenes in so many tragic, broken lives, that, as I told him, it could not be a pleasant book, that is, if it held the mirror up to life, even in only a minor and guarded degree.

However, he brought so much pressure to bear that I wrote the book. Most of it is true, though of course it was necessary to camouflage, even to minimise, the actual happenings. It was quite well received. Some reviewers applauded the courage they did not expect from a person like me, and the book sold to the extent, I believe, of about 10,000 copies.

But its effect on my usual public was very curious, in some respects disastrous. I had always been regarded as a " safe " writer, whose books could be put into the hands of young persons without any fear of deleterious consequences to the readers. Obviously, such a reputation, though comforting in parts, had its acute limitations for the purveyor of " safe " fiction. It means that the facts of life must not be faced, but ignored or covered up so that they are unsuspected. I deplore and loathe the exploitation of sex, which is the outstanding feature of modern fiction. I do not call that facing the facts in decent, sober fashion, but mere pandering to some of the baser instincts of humanity. Sex is not only the most powerful factor in human relationships, but, kept in its proper place, adds to the joy and fulfilment of life. But its proper place, in my humble opinion, is neither in the front window nor on the housetops. Moreover, it is not all of life. There are thousands in whose lives sex plays so small a part as to be almost negligible. To parade it as the only motif or inspiration is not only bad art, but absolutely untrue to life.

In *The Pendulum* I told a plain tale of the temptations and difficulties which assailed ordinary and sheltered people in the war years. I was glancing through it the other day, and marvelled that such innocuous stuff should have shocked anybody or raised a flutter in the dovecotes. But it did. It more than shocked; it alarmed my public, and they were not slow in expressing their strong disapproval. One minister's wife told me quite gravely, and with considerable unction, that she was one of a little coterie who had met together to pray that I might be restored to the right way.

Another told me that, on the Leith to London boat, a group of women had met in the saloon to discuss the book, and the finding was, " She has let us down."

I don't believe I have ever been restored to confidence or favour in these circles. But it does not keep me awake at night.

The Pendulum is a sound and true story, written out of the abundance of experience and observation, and has a definitely Christian standpoint.

The key to all this controversy, which I did not

Photo: *Francis Inglis.*

MOTHER AND DAUGHTER

ALDERSYDE, GULLANE.

find very pleasant while it lasted, is that the public sets its favourite writer in a groove from which it does not wish him or her to escape. Serial writing is a branch, almost a profession, by itself. Many first-class writers cannot write for serial publication at all. There must be no discursive meditations in a serial—the story is the thing, and if the author does not get on with it, he will have no vogue. Yet through the pages of magazines and newspapers a wider public can be reached ; a great public, which cannot afford, or which has never been educated to buy books, but which nevertheless must be fed. I have often speculated on the thrill it must be for a real best seller to behold the queues lining up to buy his latest production, to read in the publisher's lists that edition after edition is going like hot cakes. I suppose I must have sampled the sensation in a small way when *Aldersyde* was published, but it is so long ago that I think I have forgotten. I know I was glad that the book on which I had spent so many anxious days and months had found some acceptance, and been published at last.

The mainstay of my writing life has been the serial work I have done for John Leng & Co., Dundee, in the *People's Friend*. The hold of that unpretentious magazine on the public, not only in Scotland, but wherever Scots folk are to be found, is one of the romances of the newspaper world. It has no rival, though many have tried to enter the lists against it. Its public has been loyal and faithful to me for over fifty years, and there is no visible sign of waning enthusiasm even yet. The *People's Friend* has always been ably edited by men who knew their public, its limitations, and its quality. I have fitted in—that is all : and much of my best work has appeared in its pages.

This craze for serial stories, so widespread and so devouring, is very interesting from the psychological standpoint. It is meat and drink to thousands. Women, no doubt, form the main body of readers, but a good many men, I have heard, do not despise the *People's Friend*.

The late Sir Robert Donald, editor of the *Daily Chronicle* in its palmy days, told me an interesting thing at a London dinner-table one night. He disapproved of the introduction of the serial story into the columns of the daily paper, and, when he took over the editorship, part of his policy was to discontinue that feature. He allowed the one then running to run to the end, but made no provision for a successor.

To his astonishment he received a very heavy mail-bag, chiefly from women readers, bitterly complaining about the omission of the story and demanding that another should be forthcoming immediately.

We discussed this curious sidelight on a section of the newspaper public for some little time, and came to the conclusion that the chapter of the serial story supplied a felt want, a sort of dessert or titbit to the morning bacon and eggs. He drew an amusing picture of the average housewife who, having got " him " clothed and fed and dispatched, presumably in his right mind, to earn the family living, settled down with her feet on the fender to have a good, comforting hour of relaxation before she, too, tackled her day's work.

We discussed, too, how extraordinary it is that the majority of those who are avid readers of serial fiction do not want stories about people in their own rank in life. They don't mind them as subsidiary characters, and they always like the traditional family servant, ready to go through thick and thin for those he or she has served so long, even to the extent of forgoing wages, in time of family stress, but they prefer the principal characters to be people of high degree.

To any student of human nature this predilection is perfectly logical and plain. For so many the world is a drab world, in which there is not a superabundance of sunshine. " Seven shadders to one sunshine," that gentle cynic, Mark Twain, decided, no doubt, with a twinkle in his eye. Therefore, why expound or expatiate on the woes of humanity or the seamy side of life ? Trials and difficulties, of course, they must have, only to conquer and rise triumphantly above them. Wrong-doing must be punished, and innocent suffering amply rewarded. Justice must be done, too, and only the superfluous or the wicked must be allowed to die.

Among my treasures is a post card which came

to me in the far-back days, when "St. Veda's," a story of the Berwickshire coast, was running in the *People's Friend*. It bears this bitter cry in large handwriting :

" Don't let Annie Erskine die ! If you do, hanged if I read any more of your old stories."

After that, what could I do but save Annie's blameless life ?

There is a pathetic side to the almost universal demand for a happy ending. Of course it is not art, nor even true to life, in which there are so many loose ends.

But it satisfies the primal need for happiness. Denied to the reader, possibly he, or more likely she, finds some assuagement in contemplating the happiness of others in an imaginary world. So everything must be sorted up, the undeserving receive their just deserts, and the good, even if tried beyond endurance, rewarded at the end. I have never had any difficulty in adjusting myself to this demand. Because, as it happens, I feel just that way myself. The world is so full of a " number of things," many of them sad, that it does not want its burden added to by the woes of a lot of imaginary people.

It is good to show how trials may be met and conquered by courage and resource, but to me there would not be any sense in leaving the tried ones floundering in a morass.

If one has the power to act as a minor Providence, why not ?

So I am one with my readers in their love and insistence on the happy ending.

The only crow I would pick with them is that in their estimation the only really happy ending is marriage.

Whereas in real life it is only the beginning !

CHAPTER TWENTY-SEVEN

THE REWARDS OF AUTHORSHIP (II)

I HAD intended to deal with this subject in one chapter, but the material overflowed. When one is accustomed to working in a certain groove, rounding off periods and chapters within certain limits, one's thoughts somehow work automatically along these lines.

There are other rewards beside which material ones fade into insignificance.

I attribute such success as I have achieved to hard and conscientious work ; with which nothing has been allowed to interfere. I have already explained that in order that other duties and obligations to which I attached supreme importance, should not suffer, I have all my life been a very early riser, giving the morning hours, before the household was astir, to my creative work. Thus it received the freshness of the morning before the cares of the day had absorbed its pristine dew. The training at the farm helped me enormously, as in my early years I had been accustomed to rise at five in summer and six in winter. No doubt it requires some effort to sit down to one's desk at that

THE AUTHOR IN HER STUDY

discouraging hour. Many have told me they found it quite impossible.

The habit of years is still maintained. I am never later than seven of beginning my day's work, even when there is no necessity at all to keep such early hours.

Another helpful factor is that I have scrupulously observed the rules of the game, so far as Editors are concerned. They know they can depend on me to deliver the goods in time, preferably before they are needed. This has been necessary to my own peace of mind, as well as theirs. I could not write from hand to mouth, with the proverbial printer's devil behind the door. And I have honestly tried to give them what they want, realising that he who pays the piper has the right to call the tune. I am well aware that all this is anathema in literary circles, who claim, perhaps rightly, that the divine fire cannot thus be measured, chained, and regulated according to plan.

I have never had any illusions about the place accorded to me in the world of letters. Judged by some canons, it is a very low place. I shall never be recommended by the Book Society nor be allowed to consort with the elect within the guarded portals. August reviewers, who append their names to their pronouncements, would not waste a moment on any book of mine. If, by some untoward accident, it happened to alight upon their desk, it would be brushed aside as an unnecessary fly is brushed from the pane. I have not borne any grudge against

19

reviewers such as torment a good many of my fellow-craftsmen. I have never cared enough about them and don't go out of my way to read their comments. I see them accidentally rather, and on the whole have found them kind and just. This does not mean that I minimise the immense power they wield.

A great many readers take the colour of their opinions about books from the reviewers, just as thousands take their politics from the leading article in their favourite newspaper. It saves them the trouble of thinking for themselves, or of forming an independent judgment. Then there is the herd instinct. It is easier and possibly safer to run with the crowd. In the far-back days, when my second book, *Carlowrie*, was published, an intelligent, quite well-read friend expressed herself as being highly delighted with it, said that she had enjoyed it very much, and thought it far better than *Aldersyde*. A few days later, however, the *Scotsman* reviewer intimated that it was no advance on *Aldersyde*, pointing out at some length its defects. The same day I met my approving friend in the street, and she immediately referred to the notice she had read in the morning paper.

" And I liked the book so much," she said regretfully. " It just shows how one can be mistaken."

It did not occur to her to challenge the reviewer's conclusions ; she just abandoned her own without further ado. There are a good many readers of that type.

I think, however, that one of the strongest factors in such success as I have attained is the personal tie established so long ago between writer and reader, and maintained to this day. I have heard it strongly condemned by some writers, who assert that it is a hindrance rather than a help. Their contention is that you should be bold to give expression to whatever is in you, without any consideration of its effect on others. To them the public only exists as a vehicle through which they may express themselves. I am unable to dogmatise about this, though I am of opinion that only genius has the right to address mankind from such a lofty height. As genius, besides being very rare, is seldom self-assertive, when it speaks, the world stands still to listen.

The personal tie between author and reader is not rare. It has long existed in more or less degree. Dickens captured the hearts as well as the imaginations of his immense public, and has maintained it to this day.

Thackeray did not make the same personal appeal to his readers, though some who knew him intimately have told me that his personal charm and magnetism were quite exceptional.

The warm bond between me and my readers has affected my work powerfully, and I think has, in a sense, hampered it by its insistence on a certain kind of writing, for which they would accept no substitute. Had I been a different sort of woman, a stronger character, perhaps, I should not have

permitted myself to be thus enchained.   The chains
came into operation quite early in my career.

When I began to write first the market was not
overcrowded.   There were no publishers' lists so
long as to confuse, sometimes to appal.   A new
writer was an event, whereas now they are as the
sands of the sea for multitude.   The word "best
seller" had not been invented, nor any of the extraordinary methods of advertising, which fill me with
amazement not unmixed with awe.

The other day I was highly diverted to read in
a reputable literary journal that a new book by a
well-known author was to be launched at a luncheon-
party at a fashionable restaurant.

How does one launch a new book ?   Is the proverbial bottle of champagne broken on the boards
instead of on the bows to the deep-throated and
fervent music of good wishes for its safe and happy
voyaging ?

What is the meaning or portent of all this ?   Is
the cause of literature honoured and advanced by
these strange antics ?

To return to my advent as a writer.

I had the good fortune to be born in Scotland,
which is a little country, though in love for literature
it has few equals and no superiors.   It was ready
to welcome one of its own young daughters, trying
with becoming modesty to obtain a hearing.

I did not receive many letters about *Aldersyde*,
except from friends and relations.   The cult of
correspondence between author and reader was then

in its infancy. It grew, however, as time went on, and as each new book appeared, unknown friends had something to say about it through the medium of the penny post. I don't know whether personal letters have influenced me, so far as my work is concerned, but I am inclined to think they have not, to any appreciable extent. I have honestly tried to give the best in my power to the people who want to read my kind of stories, and the result has been the forging of a very warm and close personal tie about which I hesitate to write. I am aware that to help any one by their books is the last desire of certain writers. Through their gift they wish to express themselves, to air their theories and conclusions about contemporary life and the circles in which they move. The response or reaction of the reading public towards their conclusions do not trouble them in the least, except as regards sales.

I had no fixed ideas about anything when I started. I had stories to tell, which gave me no peace till they were told. The first time I met Sir James Barrie, he said he wished he had my story-telling gift. I thought he was joking at the time. Perhaps he was. To me the story is intensely real and the people in them living creatures. I suppose that is why they are so real to those who meet them in the printed page.

There are very few of my serial stories about which readers have not written, demanding a sequel, urging that they wanted to know more about the people. On only two occasions have I complied with this request, when there seemed room or justification for it.

But, generally speaking, I am ready to say good-bye to my characters when the prescribed limit has been reached, and on the outlook for the next contingent. Quite often, however, I part from them with genuine, sometimes poignant, regret.

While writing a story I live, not in an imaginary or dream world, but a very real one. I am possessed by my characters, vexed with or uplifted by them ; judging, condemning, loving them all by turns. I suppose that, in some mysterious fashion, this sense of reality is conveyed to those who read about them. Indeed it is so. Again and again I have proved it.

Some years back I had a story running in the *People's Friend* in which there were two minor characters, a woman who had been for years a faithful and devoted servant in the family whose fortunes I was writing about. She married a man called George, who had faithfully " followed " her for years. They had no children—a cross in Jess's life, for she had helped to bring up some children in the house she had left—so I thought she had better have one, just to satisfy a long-felt want. How wonderful to be able to wave the wizard's wand like this and fill up all the empty spaces !

One day a friend of mine who lived in Kirkcaldy, happened to be in the news shop in the afternoon, when the women were crowding in to buy their

MOTHER AND DAUGHTER

Friends. On the pavement one woman, eager to get the next instalment, opened out the page, and suddenly, just as my friend passed by, gave a leap into the air, crying excitedly :

" Hurrah ! Jess's gaun tae hae yin ! "

Not very long ago I happened to be opening a garden fête in the Border country. It was a beautiful summer afternoon, and after the opening was over I was preparing to depart, when I saw two women toiling up the sloping lawn, evidently in great haste. I waited, thinking they might wish to speak to me. They did. When the spokeswoman could find breath sufficient, she said :

" Eh, but we're glad you're no' away. We couldna get ower for the openin', but we've come a long wey in the bus just to ask what's gaunna happen in the story, for we canna wait."

I had some difficulty in pacifying them, for I could not at the moment recall the exact point of development in the story. However, I could assure them that all was well.

On another occasion, when I was speaking at a political meeting in Paisley to an audience of 2000 women, this note was handed up to the chairman :

" Will Mrs. Burnett Smith tell us whether Captain Hannay is going to marry Jean Adair ? "

We had some fun over it, as I solemnly charged them with bribery and corruption. The compromise arrived at was that if I heard over the wireless on the polling day that they had returned the candidate for whom I was speaking, all would be well.

He *was* returned at the top of the poll, but that is another story with which my pair of lovers had nothing to do.

Small topographical or other slips exasperate some readers so that they must write to the author offering corrections. I have had several such, some of them amusing. On one occasion I caused one of my characters to travel from Glasgow to Mauchline by the wrong railway line, and a few days after the mistake appeared, I received a letter and a penny time-table from the engine-driver of the right train convicting me of what was to him a serious breach of accuracy.

I valued that letter, because it proved that the man was really interested in the story. In the whole course of my life I have only received two spiteful anonymous letters which were immediately placed where they belonged, in the fire. It is a mystery to me what satisfaction the anonymous letter-writer gets out of his horrid achievement, since he can never know what effect it has had on his victim.

There is no doubt that the amount of public speaking I have accomplished has done a tremendous lot to strengthen, in some places to create, the personal tie. None of it was ever undertaken for that purpose. It was a quite separate and vital part of my life-work. But undoubtedly it has widened my experience and knowledge of human nature and life. One of the things I am proudest of is that the common people have heard me gladly, and that I have been assured again and again that I have helped working women, and on occasions working men, to stand up to the burden and heat of the day. If there is anything in the world more satisfying than that, I have yet to find it. The glory of the best seller fades out before it.

One day I was speaking in Glasgow to a great company of East End women whose lives, God knows, are dark enough. It may have been that I was not up to the mark myself, or that I was depressed by the hopelessness of the outlook for the great majority of those I saw in front of me. Anyhow, I seem to have spoken less cheerfully and encouragingly than usual.

Leaving the building, I had to pass through a large crowd to reach my car. Many toil-worn hands were thrust out to grasp mine, and one woman, with a shawl over her head, said unsteadily :

" Ye canna dee yet, for *we* couldna dae withoot ye."

There were no more words after that—only tears.

.   .   .   .   .   .

The love of romance is inherent in the human race. " Tell me a story ! " is one of childhood's earliest slogans.

My story-telling seems to be an inexhaustible spring.

It needs no whipping up, no wet cloths bound

about a flagging but desperate head, no retirement from the family circle, or other acute form of concentration or encouragement.

If it did, I fear that, like Grandfather's Clock, I should " stop, never to go again."

I attribute this comfortable atmosphere for work largely to the discipline of my earliest writing years.

Family life of the bracing sort puts bores in their place, faddists where they belong, and, generally speaking, scotches any attempt at superiority or conceit.

Inspiration, like idealism, is a much-abused word. Only the immortals have the right to use it.

I have quite often got my kind of inspiration for a story from a woman's face under a depressed bonnet, or been sent off on a voyage of discovery or speculation by overhearing some truculent male addressing the partner of his joys and sorrows in language such as might inspire a new essay on Is Marriage a Failure ?

The laughter that is akin to tears is never far from my lips.

For that is what life is like, marvellous web of grey and gold, which, touched by the Moving Finger, can flash or darken at will.

To the wide public which has responded for over half a century to my touch I accord my deep and heartfelt thanks. Through their aid and by their grace I have warmed both hands before the fire of life.

CHAPTER TWENTY-EIGHT

TESTAMENT OF AGE

ALTHOUGH there have been in former chapters many allusions to the religious faith which has guided and sustained me through life, it may be that some more definite pronouncement might interest some who have travelled thus far with me. I have described the kind of atmosphere in which I was bred and reared, and am now more convinced than ever that these are the years which count. There are, of course, strong individual souls which are able to rise triumphant over every handicap and to demolish barriers set up by circumstance or environment, but they will always be in the minority.

The saying attributed to the Jesuits, that the first seven years of a child's life are the moulding ones—and that the following years may be anybody's concern—contains at least a strong substratum of truth, which might well be borne in mind by those who build homes, and produce children, without much thought or consideration.

I cannot recall a time when religion, church attendance, and all the outward trappings and

expression of the Christian life were not part of
mine. But I have never undergone that strange
mental and emotional experience known as conversion. My father, like Saul of Tarsus, was
arrested by it, and it changed his whole life. With
the majority of children reared in the Christian home,
there is seldom such drastic upheaval, but rather a
growth in grace, if I may use an old-fashioned
term, not often heard in these days. As one is
gripped by life and experience, either there is confirmation of the early truths inculcated by home
and church teaching, or there is a complete break-
away. All sorts of factors, chiefly those affecting
individual experience, produce these results. It
would be difficult to describe or marshal them. It
is in strict Puritan and sectarian homes, where
there has been too much repression of natural
instincts, insistence on the gloomy rather than the
happy side of religion, that the break-away is most
common. Many prodigals as well as saints have
passed through Manse doorways.

I can remember the fierce emotional excitement
which gripped all ranks and conditions of the
people when the American evangelists, Moody and
Sankey, first visited these shores. They had a
campaign in all the large cities, and came in course
of time to Edinburgh, where we were then living.
It was a perfect orgy of revival services, even our
staid and very self-controlled mother was drawn
into the vortex and attended as many meetings as
she possibly could. Nearly all our friends and

acquaintances professed conversion and announced that they had " decided for Christ," which was the phrase used to express the passing from darkness to light. I am unable to say, at this distance, whether there was any noticeable change in our lives. I fear it was, among the members of the very young circle of which I am speaking, a purely emotional crisis through which we passed unscathed. I felt no difference in any direction. I loved the meetings, the plaintive, moving spirituals of the negro singers, the atmosphere, charged with I don't know what, but something electrical and most exciting. It was evanescent in a great many cases, though among the matured people no doubt lives were definitely changed and somewhat tepid Christianity revitalised and encouraged. I don't know what is the ultimate or permanent harvest of such revivals. I have not sufficient experience to dogmatise about them, and most certainly am the last person to pass judgment on anybody.

Each human soul has to approach its Maker by a separate road, and one person's experience is of very little use to another, either regarding religion or the other affairs of life. When one passes from the elementary stage to the deep things of life, there comes the inevitable moment when one is staggered by the contradictions and anomalies abounding in the world. You see the good and deserving passing through one misfortune after another, and the wicked flourishing apparently like the green bay tree. Confronted with the mystery and the pain of the universe, my faith sometimes shook like a reed in the wind, and my feet would falter on the Rock. It is a testing day for any sentient being, when he or she realises for the first time that all is not well with the world ; when the tragedy of suffering and frustration and injustice smites like a two-edged sword.

We consider ourselves a Christian nation and quite often proclaim it, yet permit in our midst evils which might, and could, be remedied. There is plenty for all in this fair world, yet thousands live on the borderland of starvation and misery, while thousands more have all that is best in them seared by frustration, and by witnessing the unequal distribution of wealth and beauty and grace, which they can never hope to share.

Sometimes, kept awake in the silent watches by these dark reflections, I have asked myself why God lets such things be, why He does not utter His thunder through His messengers or directly from His Heaven. But no answer comes. Apparently all that the troubled and conscience-stricken can do is to live as nearly as possible to the Christian ethic laid down by Jesus, obeying His mandate to bear one another's burdens. It would appear that in these latter days it is being slowly driven home to the minds of men that everything has failed to restore and keep sane a shattered world except the teaching of the Nazarene. Everything else has been tried—yet there is no betterment, save in the limited areas of human life and experience, where

He reigns supreme. There are gleams of light on the dark horizon ; some reaching out towards the only remedy which offers hope and release from misery and strife. If by some miracle of grace men of goodwill in every country could become of one mind in the house and should suddenly resolve to put the teaching of the Sermon on the Mount into practice in their individual, community, national, and international lives, then the problems which so far have been completely and devastatingly unsolvable would melt like mist before the rising sun.

Co-operation would take the place of competition, and the Brotherhood of Man, of which many great souls have dreamed, and for which some few have died, would become an accomplished fact.

Before that can happen there must be a change in the heart of the world, and that can only begin in the individual. If all who call themselves Christians and take His Name on their lips would surrender their worship of creeds and ceremonies, and get down to the bedrock of human need and the only remedy which can satisfy it, their influence would quickly permeate the whole body of the people, from the highest to the lowest. But they don't. They fight and argue among themselves and set up barriers and sign-posts which Jesus would be the first to demolish. Who is sufficient for these things ? They lie on my heart like a great flood.

My own personal belief is very simple. I don't

know anything about theology. It does not interest me.   The only theology which seems to be of
the slightest use is to be assured in your soul that
God exists, that He has something for you to do ;
that you are part of the Great Plan, and that if
you are in doubt, you have His Son's mandate to
guide and direct you.   There could be none more
complete, more practical, or more efficient.   It is
the cure for most of the ills to which flesh is heir.
His is a Gospel of love ; therefore, because I believe
in Him, I have tried to love my kind, and to serve
them, even when I did not like them very much.
It is easy to spend and be spent for those we love,
and who love us—no effort is needed ; and there is
always an adequate reward.   But when you try to
help people who are hostile, tiresome, suspicious, or
ungrateful, it is a different story.

But it is enormously worth while.   One's own
heart is so purged of self in the process that life
becomes a different, a more intense and lovely thing.
This does not mean that one is qualifying for
sainthood, nor that the joy of life is interfered
with.   Quite the reverse.   One's sense of humour,
one of the most powerful aids to happy living,
can always be trusted to adjust the compasses,
and especially to scotch every suggestion of self-
righteousness.   If you can see yourself as others
see you, you will be safe, nor are you forbidden the
quick, relieving flash of anger or indignation over
the incredible stupidity of the human race, beginning with yourself.

I am sure God must have a sense of humour. I don't know how He could otherwise endure the creatures He has made.

About the smug and self-righteous, who are so ready to judge others, a lot of them are good and moral merely because they have never had a chance to be anything else. Their blood runs slow, and " safety first " is the only slogan which appeals to them. I can't see life through their eyes. Some of the most lovable people I have ever known have strayed along the broad road. Surely it is worth while trying to bring them back, instead of hounding them, by cold looks and wholesale condemnation, towards the deepest declivity. Only love, human and divine, can do it.

Church life, which so much helped to mould me, has, they say, fallen on evil days. This must only be partially true. Wherever the bread is broken, the hungry are there to receive it. I can worship in any church, because creeds mean nothing to me. Every church is my Father's House where, if sought in humility and faith, He can be found. I have got much help from sermons, especially in the earlier and middle years. I remember to this day receiving help, of a very rare kind, from George MacDonald when, on my first visit to London, I toiled on foot to the heights of Highgate to hear him preach in a Congregational chapel.

Before I knew Parker intimately, I used to get much refreshment from that marvellous Sunday morning hour in the City Temple. This does not things that happen to us, outside our own folly or mistakes, we must flounder in a morass.

When the lamp of faith is early lit, much heart-burning and soul-searching are spared. I thank God that mine has never gone out, even on the darkest day. It burns more clearly now that the day is far spent than it did when the heart was young. But more and more I feel that it is the life that counts. In some very brilliant pulpits there can be found a singularly barren ministry. Those whose achievement is in no way spectacular can be as a light set on a hill. I think of one near and dear to me, the minister of a wide and very poor parish, to whom none who come seeking help and guidance are ever sent empty away.

Such are like the stars of the firmament, shining more and more unto the perfect day. We cannot all be stars, but we can see that our light, even if it looks to some nothing more than a farthing dip, at least burns clearly; especially in the zero hours of human experience, when it is necessary to call out all our reserves.

Indifference, far more than open hostility, is the present-day menace to religion. People are not interested—there are too many other distractions in a hectic world, where the prevailing creed seems to be " Let us eat and drink, and be merry, for to-morrow we die." Nothing can shake or challenge that deadly wall except some desperate need.

When all else fails and friends are few, the human heart begins to turn, with a strange, wistful longing,